Inside the World of a Football Agent

Inside the World of a Football Agent

Gennaro Giulio Tedeschi

BEP

BUSINESS EXPERT PRESS

Leader in applied, concise business books

Inside the World of a Football Agent

Cover design by Charlene Kronstedt

Interior design by Exeter Premedia Services Private Ltd., Chennai, India

First published in 2021 by
Business Expert Press, LLC
222 East 46th Street, New York, NY 10017
www.businessexpertpress.com

ISBN-13: 978-1-63742-036-2 (paperback)
ISBN-13: 978-1-63742-037-9 (e-book)

Business Expert Press Sports and Entertainment Management Collection

Collection ISSN: 2333-8644 (print)
Collection ISSN: 2333-8652 (electronic)

First edition: 2021

10 9 8 7 6 5 4 3 2 1

To my loved ones: Amanda, Roberta, Mom & Dad.

Description

In the forward 2021, FIFA (Federation Internationale de Football Association) will significantly innovate the figure of one of the most important protagonists of the football world: the football agent.

Inside the World of a Football Agent provides a series of practical cases, experienced first-hand by the author, that will help the readers to immerse themselves in the reality of a football agent that interacts with presidents, CEO, sports directors, supporters, footballers, and their families. In an ever-increasing need for professionalization, the author, thanks to his background in representing footballers, presents a clear analysis of the current international regulation and its latest regulatory innovations.

The audience for the book is represented by all the current or aspiring professionals involved in the football industry: from football agents who want to keep up to date with the latest legislation, to aspiring agents, sports directors or media, who want to understand what is often behind a yes or no in a complicated transfer negotiation. The book will also be of interest to graduate schools of business, sports, marketing, and MBA programs in law.

Keywords

Football agent; intermediary; football; soccer; FIFA; entrepreneurship; football industry; football transfer market; sports law; football law; international business; business professionals; sports management

Contents

Introduction xi

Chapter 1   From the "FIFA regulation on working with
             intermediaries" to the New FIFA Agents Regulation
             Reform of 2021 1
Chapter 2   Comparative Examination of the Figure of the
             Football Agent in the European "Big Five Sisters"
             and Its Historical Excursus 33
Chapter 3   The Peculiar Regulation of the Football
             Agents in the USA 67
Chapter 4   How to Become a Football Agent: Practical Examples 103
Chapter 5   Manage Relationships with the Players' Families,
             Medias, and Colleagues 117

About the Author 131
Index 133

Introduction

The Football Agent: A Hybrid Figure,
a Professional or a Practical One

A dichotomic relationship has characterized this profession since its genesis precisely due to the very strong personal component in the performance of the activity itself by the service provider, the agent indeed.

Brokerage activity is certainly a historical phenomenon, but it is constantly growing in professional sport and football in particular. In 2019 alone (the 2020 annuity cannot be considered, considering that has not ended yet at the time of writing), in football, the fees paid to agents exceeded 548 million dollars, while in 2013 the value of the fees was less than a third of this figure.

The aim of this book is to deepen, both through a timely study of the sector legislation, and following some practical cases put in place by the author of this text, the figure of the football agent. The regulatory history of the football agent that will be dealt with in this text, will focus on the figure and evolution of sports agent, limited to the football players agents, the so called *football agents*, as mentioned in several FIFA regulations that have taken place over thirty years. In particular, in Chapter 1, attention will first be paid to a critical analysis of the international regulations, analyzed in a natural chronological order of publication of the acts by FIFA, passing on a comparative examination of the figure of the football agent between the five major European football federations, "The Big Five sisters," in Chapter 2. Considering the regulatory framework that is mostly common to each other, as it is straight imposed by FIFA on the individual national sports federations, through the text, it will become clear how the analysis will move from an economic and socio-demographic point of view, rather than a purely legal one.

Chapter 3 will cover a careful analysis of the U.S. Soccer Federation's agent regulations, which will be followed by an analysis on the soccer phenomenon in the United States and on why the most practiced sport in the world is still far behind in the American sports hierarchies.

The normative approach of the text that introduces us to the discussion of the matter of the players' agent on a legal level, already at the end of the Chapter 3, comes to an end giving space in the Chapter 4, to the treatment of practical experiential cases personally experienced by the author of the book, and useful advice on how to deal with all the possible situations in which you may find yourself being a players' agent.

Finally, the fifth chapter will at first try to provide a guidance on how to manage relations with the world of the media and the footballer's family. The chapter in question, however, does not have the presumption of being a holy bible on how to manage the already delicate inter-family relationships of the player, but simply through lived situations, tries to build, case by case, a possible series of alternative paths to follow together with his client, in case the sporting aspect of his career does not go as planned. Finally, the last chapter will focus on the relationship, very often underestimated between the various agents, sharks that swim in the same sea, and therefore, as such, have had to learn to collaborate.

CHAPTER 1

From the "FIFA regulation on working with intermediaries" to the New FIFA Agents Regulation Reform of 2021

Who is a Football agent?

According to the FIFA Regulation on Players' agent of October 29, 2007, the football agent is

> a natural person who, for a fee, introduces players to clubs with a view to negotiating or renegotiating an employment contract or introduces two clubs to one another with a view to concluding a transfer agreement, in compliance with the provisions set forth in these regulations.

FIFA has regulated, or tried to regulate, the figure of the football agents since its first appearance in the football field.

The main stepping stones of the regulation of the football agent's figure are:

- The original regulation
- The amended regulation
- The Blatter reform
- New prospectuses of reform

The analysis covered by this work can therefore only start from one of the regulatory cornerstones of the international federation, namely the FIFA Statute, focusing in particular on Article 2,[1] which peremptorily enshrines the objectives of the Fédération Internationale de Football Association (hereinafter FIFA). FIFA[2] aims to:

> constantly improve the game of football and spread it throughout the world taking into account its universal, educational, cultural and humanitarian impact, putting into practice development programs aimed in particular at young people; organize their international competitions; establish rules and ensure that they are respected; control the game of football in all its forms, taking all necessary or advisable measures to prevent violation of the Statute, regulations, decisions of FIFA and the Regulations of the game; to prevent certain methods and practices from compromising the integrity of the game or competitions or from involved in abuses in the context of the game of football.

The Recognition of Football Agents

The recognition of footballers' agents as a well-established figure in the world of football, both at national and international level, together with a regulatory apparatus provided by FIFA statutes and individual national

---

[1] Art. 2 FIFA Regulations on working with Intermediaries 2015:"... in the selection and engaging process of intermediaries, players and clubs shall act with due diligence. In this context, due diligence means that platers and clubs shall use reasonable endeavours to ensure that the intermediaries sign the relevant Intermediary Declaration and the Representation contract concluded between the parties."

[2] The Fédération Internationale de Football Association, better known by the acronym FIFA, is the international federation that governs the sports of football, five-a-side football and beach soccer. Its headquarters are located in Zurich, Switzerland. The federation was founded in Paris on May 21, 1904 and is responsible for organizing all intercontinental events. The six different confederations (officially recognized by the federation), which are responsible for organizing and supervising football activities in the various continents of the world AFC, CAF, CONCACAF, CONMEBOL, OFC, UEFA, all belong to FIFA.

football federations, certainly appear to be the essential elements that have led FIFA itself to create a set of rules to regulate the activities of the agents. The International Federation, in fact, has recognized almost immediately (since their first appearance in the world of football) the figure of the agents as a professional category, and has remained constant in this approach (until the reform, which will shortly be discussed in depth, intervened on April 1, 2015), officially recognizing this figure with the decision of the FIFA Executive Committee of May 20, 1994. According to FIFA, among the considerations that accompanied the decision to regulate the activities of footballers' agents, that there is first and foremost the need to protect those most directly concerned and therefore exposed to this activity, namely footballers, in order to guarantee them as much professional assistance as possible. If we divide the legal evolution of this profession, we could talk about three phases. In the initial phase, FIFA was convinced of the certain and necessary professionalism of the category of football agents, which therefore saw as a logical consequence its official recognition, sanctioned by the entry into force of the first rules of procedure dated May 20, 1994, amended on 11 December, 1995, and entered into force on January 1, 1996 (the *initial Regulation*). FIFA regulated, in fact, the access to the profession through the direct issue of the license conditional on a completely discretionary analysis of the applicant's profile by its federation and the payment of a bank guarantee of CHF 200,000 to the international federation. Anyone who had seen their application accepted could apply next to his name, the qualification of "FIFA Players' Agent."

The Original Regulation and its application problems: The "Piau" and Multiplayers International Denmark cases (and proceedings)

Toward the end of the last century, competition proceedings were opened against FIFA by the European Commission on the basis of a complaint that considered the FIFA regulation to be contrary to the provisions of the EC Treaty precisely in Article 100a of the Treaty 144 on free competition because of excessive restrictions on the excess of the profession. The original Regulation made the exercise of that profession subject, in fact, to the possession of a license issued by the competent national federation and reserved the activity in question for natural persons (Articles 1 and 2). Prior to obtaining the license, an interview was held to test the candidate's knowledge, particularly legal and sporting knowledge (Articles 6, 7, and 8). The latter also had to satisfy certain requirements of compatibility and morality, such as the absence of criminal convictions in criminal records (Articles 2, 3, and 4). The professional who wanted to be defined and recognized as football agent also had to deposit, as already mentioned, a bank guarantee of 200,000 Swiss francs (CHF) (Article 9). The contract governing the relationship between the agent and the player could last a maximum of two years but was renewable (Article 12). Agents, players, and clubs that broke the rules would be variously sanctioned. Staff could, by a security, censure, or warning, impose an unspecified fine and withdraw their license (Article 14). Players and clubs, could be fined up to CHF 50,000 and CHF 100,000, respectively. Players could also be imposed the disciplinary sanction of suspension from competitive sport (up to 12 months), clubs could be suspended or prohibited from any transfer (Articles 16 and 18). A "Footballer's Status Commission" was designated as FIFA's supervisory and decision-making body (Article 20).

On March 23, 1998, an agent of the Federation Francaise de Football (FFF) footballers, Mr. Piau lodged a complaint[3] with the Commission concerning the abovementioned initial Regulation. He complained, first, that the regulation was contrary to Article 10 of the Directive of the European Commission that foresees that "It is for the national court to ensure that, in the light of the provisions of Article 49 and the following articles of the Treaty relating to the freedom to provide services, the restrictions on the exercise of the profession consisting of the opaque examination procedures and the obligation to guarantee banking and, on the other hand, the provision for supervision and penalties." Secondly, the complaint considered that the regulation could lead to discrimination between Member States. Thirdly, it was complained that the Regulation did not provide for the means of judicial protection or appeal of the applicable decisions and penalties.

---

[3] See Judgment of the Court of First Instance of the European Communities, Cause T-193/02, Piau / Commission of the European Communities, in "Rivista di Legge ed Economia dello Sport," n. 1, 2005, 127 et seq.

Even before that, on February 20, 1996, the Commission received a complaint from Multiplayers International Denmark, which questioned the compatibility of the same Staff Regulations with Articles 25 and 19 of the Treaty. The Commission can also support Amendments Nos 81[4] EC and 82[5] EC, which are also related to the freedom of competition

---

[4] Article 81 EC: "Treaty of Rome": 1. All agreements between companies, all decisions by associations of companies and all concerted practices which may affect trade between Member States and which have as their basis are incompatible with the common market object or effect of preventing, restricting or distorting competition within the common market and in particular those consisting in: (a) directly or indirectly fixing purchase or sale prices or other transaction conditions, (b) limiting o control production, outlets, technical development or investments, (c) share markets or sources of supply, (d) apply, in commercial relations with other contractors, dissimilar conditions for equivalent services, so as to determine for the latter a competitive disadvantage, (e) making the conclusion of contracts conditional on the acceptance by the other parties of additional services, which, by their nature or according to commercial usage, have no connection with the object of the contracts themselves. 2. Agreements or decisions prohibited by virtue of this article are automatically void. 3. However, the provisions of paragraph 1 may be declared inapplicable: - to any agreement or category of agreements between undertakings, - to any decision or category of decisions of associations of undertakings, and - to any concerted practice or category of concerted practice which contribute to improving the production or distribution of products or to promoting technical or economic progress, while reserving users a fair share of the resulting profit, and avoiding (a) imposing restrictions on the undertakings concerned that are not indispensable for achieving these objectives (b) to give such undertakings the possibility of eliminating competition in respect of a substantial part of the products in question.

[5] Articolo 82 CE: "Trattato di Roma": Any abuse by one or more undertakings of a dominant position within the common market or in a substantial part of it shall be prohibited as incompatible with the common market insofar as it may affect trade between Member States. Such abuse may, in particular, consist in: (a) directly or indirectly imposing unfair purchase or selling prices or other unfair trading conditions; (b) limiting production, markets or technical development to the prejudice of consumers; (c) applying dissimilar conditions to equivalent transactions with other trading parties, thereby placing them at a competitive disadvantage; (d) making the conclusion of contracts subject to acceptance by the other parties of supplementary obligations which, by their nature or according to commercial usage, have no connection with the subject of such contracts.

in professionalization. The Commission has also informed of petitions introduced before the European Parliament by citizens of German and French nationality, declared admissible by the European Parliament on October 29, 1996 and March 9, 1998, respectively, also relating to the rules under discussion. The Commission thus opened proceedings in accordance with Council Regulation No 17 of February 6, 1962, first Regulation implementing Articles (81) and (82) of the Treaty (OJ 1962, No. 13, p. 204), and notified FIFA of a statement of objections on October 19, 1999. That notice defined the regulation (the so-called initial regulation) as a decision of the association of undertakings within the meaning of Article 81 EC and called into question the compatibility with that provision of the restrictions contained in that Regulation, namely the mandatory nature of the license, the exclusion of its attribution to legal persons, the prohibition on clubs and players from using unauthorized agents, the demand for a bank guarantee, and the provision of sanctions. On January 4, 2000, in response to the statement of objections, FIFA contested that the abovementioned regulation could be called an *association decision* instead of a regulation. A decision was more an expression of a political enclave, it was not as effectively binding as a regulation. In order to justify the restrictions the decision entailed, FIFA claimed "an anxiety about the moralization and qualification of the profession" and argued that it was possible to derogate from it on the basis of Article 100a of the Treaty. 81, point 3, EC.

The "amended" Regulation of March 1, 2001 and the closing of the "Piau case"

Following the administrative procedure initiated by the Commission, FIFA adopted on December 10, 2000 a new regulation for the activities of the football agents, which entered into force on March 1, 2001 and was again amended on April 3, 2002. The new FIFA Regulation (*the amended regulation*) maintains the obligation, necessary to practice the profession of the player agent (which continues to be reserved to natural persons) to hold a license issued by the competent national federation for an unlimited period (Articles 1, 2, and 10). In addition, in the amended regulation, other than having an *impeccable reputation* (Article 2), the candidate must undergo a written examination (Articles 4 and 5), in the form of a multiple-choice questionnaire, aimed at verifying their legal and sporting knowledge. The candidate must also provide professional liability insurance or, in alternative, deposit a bank guarantee amounting to CHF 100,000 (Articles 6 and 7). The relationship between the agents and the players they wish to represent must be enshrined in a written contract of up to two years, which is renewable. The contract must provide for the remuneration of the agent, which is calculated on the basis of the player's gross basic remuneration and fixed, unless otherwise agreed by the parties, to the extent of 5 percent of the same. A copy of the contract must be sent to the national federation, which keeps a register of the contracts received and that is always available at FIFA headquarters (Article 12). Authorized agents must, inter alia, comply with FIFA's statutes and regulations and cannot approach a player who is under contract with a company (Article 14). Finally, there is a series of sanctions against clubs, players, and agents included in this amended version too. All of the above are, in fact, liable, if they break the mentioned rules, to a security, censure, or warning, as well as fines (Articles 15, 17, and 19). Agents may be required to suspend or withdraw their license (Article 15); players may risk a suspension for up to 12 months (Art. 17); clubs may also be suspended and prohibited from moving their players for at least three months (Article 19); fines can be imposed on everyone, football agents and clubs. The amount of the fine for the agents is not specified (as it was not in the original regulation), whereas for players and clubs, it is now at least 10,000 or 20,000 Swiss francs respectively (Articles 15, 17, and 19 respectively). Penalties may be imposed jointly (Articles 15, 17, and 19). In the event of disputes, the national federation concerned or the "Footballer's Status Commission" (Article 22) shall have jurisdiction. Transitional measures allow the validation of licenses granted in accordance with the old legislation (Article 23). A code of professional conduct and a standard model representative contract (Annexes B and C respectively) are also annexed to the amended Regulation. The amendments made on April 3, 2002, specify that citizens of the European Union (EU) or the European Economic Area (EEA) must refer the license application to the national federation of their country or country of residence, regardless of the length of their residence, and will be able to take out the insurance policy prescribed in any country of the European Union or the EEA. On July 9 and 10, 2001, the European Parliament declared the files closed.

On August 3, 2001, the Commission sent Mr. Piau a letter pursuant to Article 6 of Commission Regulation (EC) No 2842 of December 22, 1998 on hearings in certain proceedings under Articles (81) and (82) of the EC Treaty (OJ L 354, p. 18). The Commission stated that its intervention at FIFA had led to the elimination of the most restrictive measures contained in the "Regulation for the activities of players' agents" and that there was no longer any interest on the part of the Community in following up the proceedings.

On November 12, 2001, the Commission sent a similar letter to Multiplayers International Denmark, to which the company did not reply.

Mr. Piau informed the Commission that, even considering their lack of interest in pursuing the proceedings, he was maintaining the complaint. He claimed that infringements of Article 81(1) EC in respect of examination and professional insurance remained in the amended Regulation and that new infringements had been introduced in the form of ethical rules, standard contract models and methods of calculating remuneration. Those restrictions, in his view, could not be avoided by a derogation under Article 81(3) EC. The applicant then claimed that the Commission had not examined the contested regulation in the light of the wording of Article 82 EC.

By decision of April 15, 2002, the Commission rejected Mr. Piau's complaint.

According to the institution, there was insufficient Community interest to follow up the procedure since the more restrictive provisions complained of had been repealed. With regards to the mandatory nature of the license, it could be justified—and those that remained could have been derogated on the basis of Article 81(3) EC and Article 82 EC did not apply in the present case. The European Commission decided to close the proceedings when FIFA agreed to amend its rules, giving rise to a second phase, characterized by a massive proliferation of rules regarding football agents.

The second phase was the result of a long period during which the legal basis for the figure of the player agent were defined. The new FIFA regulation, entered into force on March 1, 2001 (revised several times in the years: 2006, 2009, 2011) with radical regulatory changes, including the obligation for the aspiring agent to pass an exam in the form of a multiple choice written questionnaire and the obligation to take out civil liability insurance in order to obtain the license for an unlimited period by the competent national federation and no longer FIFA. One of the most impactful consequences, much more cultural than factual, was the suppression of the term "FIFA Players' Agent," the use of which is still widespread today especially among those who obtained the license at the dawn of the different regulation. Today, the use of the term constitutes a violation of the protected brand of the World Football Federation. Through this regulation, once the license had been purchased by the national federation, the agent is entitled to use the title of "Players' Agent Licensed by the X Football Association." Subsequently, the exponential and, in some ways, disorderly growth of the profession at international level, and above all, the increasing number of appeals to the courts of the highest body in international football (in order to settle disputes between agents, footballers, and clubs) led FIFA to amend and revise more restrictively its rules on football agents.

The Blatter Reform

The "Blatter reform" named after the former FIFA president, the same one who had in fact signed the previous regulation of the figure in question, evolved the role and legal qualification of the footballers' agent radically in April 2015. In fact, the figure in question has been completely transformed into a *sports intermediary*. The new regulation, in essence, no longer restricts access to the profession and, as stated on FIFA's official website in April 2015,

> is based on principles of transparency, with regard to the activity of intermediaries, and good administration of federations that will have the task of creating national registers and adopting regulations transposing FIFA principles.

This gaunt and imprecise regulation has led to many problems from the point of view of the application of legislation, which suddenly was no longer harmonized by any central body of the ball, as it was before with FIFA, a body which is a homologator of rules par excellence in the field of football. This gives rise to a series of practical iniquities in the performance of the profession of football agents, depending on whether the profession was carried out in a nation that had confined itself only to incorporating the FIFA regulation into its essential points rather than to another that had decided to *supplement* these minimum requirements dictated by the Zurich body (FIFA). In Italy, Germany, and Portugal, for example, this has led to the introduction of the *double representation* rule, which is typical of brokerage, since it is now the market operator suddenly projected into a sector where it should no longer have been in the interests of either of the two parties involved in a negotiation, but of both.

The new name of *intermediary* brings with it, on a practical level, two other important regulatory innovations: the first, to be an intermediary, comes without distinction among a natural or legal person, who will have to register with a registration system held by the individual National Sports Federation, communicating both the activities carried out and the compensation received; the second (and in some ways symptomatic of a clear and more general position of indifference or mere tolerance of the newly formed intermediary figure assumed by FIFA), FIFA implicitly states that it no longer wishes to deal, in the event of a violation of disciplinary rules or rules by the intermediary, with the resolution of all future disputes between intermediary and footballer, or intermediary and company. FIFA itself, on the other hand, will, as it has always been, penalize the player or club who have appointed the intermediary for the single operation in dispute. The profession also changes from the point of view of the total remuneration due to an intermediary to represent a footballer, and the way in which he is wound up. In fact, the percentage allocated to the services rendered by the intermediary may not exceed 3 percent of the player's basic gross income for the entire duration of the contract. The principles that led FIFA to do so are therefore formally inspired by the transparency of the operations and the containment of costs by the companies. In practice, however, as I have said, the reform has resulted in the liberalization of the profession and a reduction in the requirements for access. This decision has caused great alarm in the category of agents of FIFA-licensed footballers that, according to the most recent census dated

Table 1.1 Number of licensed agents

Nation	Number of FIFA licensed Agents
Italy	1,063
Spain	560
England	557
Germany	482
Argentina	225
Brazil	203
Other countries	148

2017, are 6,501 in the world and only in Italy, which holds the record, as many as 1,063, followed by Spain with 560, England with 557, Germany with 482, Argentina 225, Brazil 203, and gradually all the other countries represented that are 148 (Table 1.1).

The FIFA Regulation on Intermediaries 2015, therefore, currently presents structural and regulatory critical issues that need a more in-depth analysis in their key points.

The Regulation, in fact, reaffirms the role of the intermediary who is defined as:

A natural or legal person who for a fee or free of charge, represents players and/or clubs in negotiations, in order to conclude a Contract, or represents the clubs in negotiations to conclude a Transfer Agreement

and the tasks of the Federations, in Article 19 titled as *Purpose*.

In fact, national bodies are required to consider the provisions of the regulation as minimum principles on which their federal internal legislation should be based.

In Article 2, with particular reference to paragraph 2, FIFA, on the other hand, requires clubs and players to choose intermediaries diligently and in compliance with the requirements laid down with regard to the representative contract and the declaration of intermediation. Article 3 states that the intermediary chosen for the individual transaction must be registered and have an impeccable reputation with the characteristics prescribed by Article 4 entitled "Requisites for Registration." The qualification of *impeccable* has origins from Article 6 paragraph 1 of the previous FIFA Football agents Regulation approved by the FIFA Executive Committee on October 29, 2007, and entered into force on January 1, 2008, where the *impeccable reputation* was even considered as a prerequisite for access to the qualification examination for the profession of the agent, and therefore, inserted in the wider Article 6 entitled "Preliminary requirements for submitting an application." According to this rule, impeccable reputation corresponds to not having received criminal convictions for financial crimes or violent crimes. Important news compared to the previous regulation, dated 2006, was also introduced with regard to the right to compensation, here provided for in commission mode and proportional to gross compensation, but calculated over the entire duration of the contract concluded by the professional footballer, as provided for in Article 7 paragraph 314 and no longer commensurate with the individual annuity. The amount of remuneration due to an intermediary acting in the interest of a player must be calculated on the basis of the fixed part of the gross total engagement for the entire duration of the contract. Clubs that use the services of an intermediary will have to pay for it with the payment of a lump sum, agreed before the conclusion of the transaction. With the agreement of all the parties, the payment can also be paid in installment solution. Taking into account the national regulations and national and international mandatory rules, Article 7(3)(a)(b)(c) provides an indication of how to pay compensation to the intermediary, as a recommendation, establishing that players and clubs may adopt the following benchmarks: the fixed part of the gross total engagement, calculated for the entire duration of the sports performance contract; (b) the total amount of remuneration due to the intermediary who has acted in the interest of a club in the conclusion of a contract with a player should not exceed three per cent (3%) the fixed part of the gross total engagement, calculated for the entire duration of the sports performance contract; (c) the total amount of remuneration due to the intermediary acting in the interest of the club for the conclusion of a transfer agreement should not exceed three per cent (3%) of the amount paid for the player's transfer. Clubs must ensure that payments made from one club to another in connection with the transfer, variable part of the engagement, training compensation,[6]

---

[6] The Training Compensation: Article 20 FIFA Regulations on the Status and Transfer of Players, consists in the payment of a sum—defined as a parameter—to clubs that have trained young players, which accrues upon signing a multi-year membership. The objective of this regulation is to develop the training of young players and more generally to reward clubs that deal exclusively with the youth sector. The FIFA preparation and conception award (the FIFA Player Status and Transfer Regulations govern the institution, calling it the training allowance), together with the solidarity mechanism, constitute the forms of "incentive" for the development of youth football. In order to economically quantify the accruing prizes, FIFA divides the clubs into 4 categories according to the Championship and the Confederation to which they belong. The payment of this indemnity accrues upon signing the first contract as a professional or upon subsequent transfers within the age of 23. Therefore, the clubs "eligible for compensation" according to the provisions of Annex 4 to the FIFA Regulations on the Status and Transfers of Players, are those that have contributed to the training of the player between 12 and 23 years of age. The same article, also the cases in which the payment of this indemnity is not due, that is: If the registration of the player is carried out by an amateur club or by a club belonging to the fourth category in the national system of categorization of clubs; or if the registration of the player took place following a termination of the contract for just cause between the player himself and the previous club, without prejudice to the rights of the previous clubs that formed the player. The payment of the training allowance must be made within 30 days from the registration of the player. The club or clubs that have not received the payment of this award within 18 months of their registration can lodge a complaint with the FIFA Dispute Resolution Chamber (CRC) at the first instance and possibly at the second instance at the CAS in Lausanne. After 18 months without any request for payment of the training allowance, or in the event of bankruptcy of the club or clubs that contributed to the player's training, the prize will be paid to the federation/s of the countries in which the same player was formed. The National Sports Federation is then obliged to use these fees for the future training of "young amateur" or "non-professional" young players of players who in the previous season had been registered as "young" with an annual bond, are required to pay the cd to the club or clubs for which the player has previously been registered. "Preparation bonus" on the basis of a parameter, doubled in the case of club membership of the professional leagues, updated at the end of each sporting season based on the ISTAT cost of living indexes, except

or solidarity mechanism,[7] are not paid to intermediaries and that such payments are not made by the intermediaries.[8] This prohibition also

---

in the case where the request concerns clubs belonging to the same league. A key aspect is that the player's bond, for at least an entire football season, is an essential condition for the right to the prize.

[7] Solidarity mechanism: Article 21 FIFA Regulations on the Status and Transfer of Players, and Annex 6 of the same regulations: According to the two rules in question, "If a professional football player transfers during a contract, 5 percent of any remuneration, with the exception of training, paid to the previous club, must be deducted from the total of these fees and distributed by the destination club as a solidarity contribution to the club(s) that have provided the player with training and education over the years. This solidarity contribution takes into account the number of years (calculated in proportion if less than one year) during which the player was registered for the club / clubs in question in the seasons between the 12th and 23rd year of age." The contribution is equivalent to 5 percent of the price agreed by the two companies for the transfer according to the established rates. Therefore, the destination club must pay the solidarity contribution to the teams that are entitled to the compensation. This percentage must be deducted from the total transfer, and therefore would be borne by the transferring company. Therefore, each club for which the player has been registered from 12 to 23 years of age is entitled to a share according to the scheme presented in the table above. This cost is charged to the income statement, among other charges, by the company that supports it. The FIFA regulations also indicate the payment terms, specifying that "The destination club is required to pay the solidarity contribution to the club(s) that have provided the player with the training in accordance with the provisions of this Annex no later than 30 days from the player's registration or, in the case of installment payments, within 30 days from the date of the individual payments." Furthermore, always according to the rules, "If it is not possible to establish a link between the professional player and some of the clubs that formed him within 18 months of the transfer, the solidarity contribution must be paid to the Federation(s) of the country (or countries) in which the professional received his training. This contribution will be earmarked for youth football development programs in the Federation (or Federations) in question." "Solidarity contribution and training allowance: However, the solidarity contribution mechanism is not to be confused with the training allowance. The training allowance is paid on the occasion of the first contract as a professional and for transfers up to 23 years of age. While the solidarity contribution must be paid for each single transfer for consideration in the manner described above."

[8] Article 7.4 FIFA Regulations on working with Intermediaries 2015: "Clubs shall ensure that payments to be made by one club to another club in connection

refers, but not only, to any additional rights to the variable part of the engagement or the future transfer value of a player. The transfer of credit is also prohibited. According to the provisions of Article 7 paragraph 6,[9] any payment due for the services of an intermediary must be made exclusively by the intermediary's client to the intermediary himself. After the conclusion of the transaction and with the consent of the club, the player may provide his written consent for the club to pay the intermediary in his name. The payment made by the club on behalf of the player must comply with the manner previously agreed between the player and the intermediary. Officers,[10] as defined in paragraph 11 of the Definitions section of the FIFA Statute, are prohibited from receiving from an intermediary the total sum or part of it, due to that intermediary for a transaction. The officer who contravenes this provision will be subject to disciplinary sanctions. Finally, Article 8 states that for

> players and/or clubs who use the advice of an intermediary in the negotiation of a sports performance contract and/or a transfer agreement, it is forbidden to pay any payment to the intermediary, if the player concerned is a minor, as defined in point 11 of the Definitions section of the FIFA Regulation on status and transfers of the players.

---

with a transfer, such as transfer compensation, training compensation or solidarity contributions, are not paid to intermediaries and that the payment is not made by intermediaries. This includes, but is not limited to, owning any interest in any transfer compensation or future transfer value of a player. The assignment of claims is also prohibited."

[9] Article 7.6 FIFA Regulations on working with Intermediaries 2015: "After the conclusion of the relevant transaction and subject to the club's agreement, the player may give his written consent for the club to pay the intermediary on his behalf. The payment made on behalf of the player shall be in accordance with the terms of payment agreed between the player and the intermediary."

[10] Article 7.7 FIFA Regulations on working with Intermediaries 2015: "Officials, as defined in point 11 of the Definitions section of the FIFA Statutes, are prohibited from receiving any payment from an intermediary of all or part of the fees paid to that intermediary in a transaction. Any official who contravenes the above shall be subject to disciplinary sanctions."

Analyzing FIFA's reform of football agents, so-called deregulation, is a difficult task because, in the opinion of the writer, there is no reading that leads the interpreter to identify an acceptable rationale.

The Blatter reform has its roots in an industry study wanted by the Zurich Federation itself, which revealed that the agents' fees reached 254 million dollars in the period 2011 through 2013, only 14.6 percent of the value of the 865 deals in which prosecutors were present (worth 1.7 billion dollars[11]). The same study also shows that 83 percent of these commissions were produced by operations within UEFA. Such a low percentage is a clear sign that the intention to professionalize a figure such as that covered by this work, by FIFA and individual national sports federations, has failed. However, perhaps the quickest path was pursued, that of implementing a *free all policy*, through this centralized deregulation which, in fact, proved to be the wrong choice. In fact, in the period since April 1, 2015, the day on which the new regulation "FIFA regulations on working with intermediaries" became effective, not only has there been an exponential increase in the number of intermediaries, but the lack of addition by the majority of the individual sports federations, the so-called "Minimum Standards," has provoked a proliferation of judicial appeals against figures without competence, preparation and, above all, guarantees, provided for in the previous FIFA regulations, such as the obligation to take out insurance policies, leaving the world of football, the third sector of the world economy, as often non-stick characters, and therefore, toward whom nothing was appropriate in a vain attempt to counter illegal actions or against any federal regulation. Furthermore, "deregulation" has had the effect to act as a diaspora of regulations, in an increasingly global and multicultural market, which goes beyond national borders (and lives and is intertwined with international rights) lacking any reference whatsoever to regulatory harmonization between the relevant rules in individual States.

In a time when all sectors of public life, the labor market in particular, choose to sectorize skills in order to increase professionalism and quality

---

[11] Il Sole 24 ore, Marco Bellinazzo, 4th March 2013,—calciomercato UEFA "solidale": In the period between 2011\2013, turnover of 5.1 billion euros, more than half towards smaller clubs.

standards of performance, the world of football decided to backtrack and clear, with ad hoc regulation, improvisation, and self-certified competence on a pre-printed form.

We have paradoxically moved from an internationally and nationally regulated activity, that while presenting completely fillable gaps guaranteed a minimum common level of professional preparation certified by passing an enabling exam, to a free square where, paying the secretarial rights equal to €500.00 for registration in the Register and €150.00 for each *representation contract* deposited, it is legitimate to claim the right to qualify themselves as *Intermediary* and represent players and clubs without guaranteeing knowledge of the basic regulations and the related technical aspects provided with regard to the memberships, transfers, and contracts of footballers with related protections. In this international regulatory chaos, it has certainly played an important and harmonizing role within the Community, the European Commission. As above mentioned, the Commission's discussions with FIFA in 2001 led to the amendment of FIFA's rules on player status and transfer. The 2009 study on sports agents in the European Union analyzed the activities of agents and their wider role, in the context of the internationalization of professional sport. An EU conference on sports agents focusing on the main team sports in Europe took place in 2011 and identified the standardization of the profession as an option for further consultation and an opportunity to develop and test the quality requirements of the profession. In 2013, the Commission published a study on the economic and legal aspects of player transfers, which shows that transfer systems adopted by clubs can help ensure fairer competition.

Future Reform Prospectuses

On September 26, 2018, FIFA announced the decision of the FIFA Football Stakeholders Committee[12] meeting in London, to carry out a reform, as a result of a series of meetings between the FIFA Football

---

[12] Football Stakeholders Committee: advises and assists the Council on all football-related matters, in particular on the structure of the game, as well as on all technical matters. The committee will also address the relationship between

Stakeholders Committee with ECA,[13] the Leagues (in particular the World Leagues Forum), the Players' Association (FIFpro) and numerous Federations and Confederations. The aim of this reform is to improve the transparency of the system of transfers of footballers and, to this end, it has identified prosecutors as the focus of this system. One of the most interesting parts of the transfer reform concerns intermediaries, which will see a significant new change after those of 2010 and 2015. Since 2015, FIFA (FIFA Circular No. 1417), has implemented deregulation, which has liberalized access to the profession of agent/intermediary, abolishing licenses and the possibility for intermediaries to represent multiple parties. In addition, it excluded the competence of the International Sports Organization (Player Status Committee) and the state law of each individual FIFA member state in matters of disputes concerning intermediaries. The implementation of this scheme devised by FIFA has been delegated to the national federations that have implemented it differently; for example, Italy first accepted deregulation and then provided, by a law of the State, the creation of the figure of the sports agent (Article 1 paragraph 373 of law 27 December 2017 n. 205) and of the d.p.c.m. of March 23, 2018. Italy, in freeing the sporting system from the exclusivity of competence, took its cue from the FFF (France Football Federation), which pioneered the activity of football agents first with a state law. The 2015 system appeared incomplete and, since last April, has led FIFA to

---

clubs, players, leagues, affiliated associations, confederations, and FIFA, as well as matters relating to the interests of football clubs around the world.

[13] ECA (European Club Association) is a body that represents football clubs at European level. The purpose of the ECA is to protect and promote football in Europe. Article 2 letter a of the 2017 ECA Statute, available on www.ecaeurope.com, states that "The objectives of ECA are: To safeguard and promote the interests of European club football, in particular, and club football in general." The ECA was created to replace the G-14, an organization that dissolved in January 2008 as well as the UEFA European Clubs Forum and is chaired by Karl-Heinze Rumenigge. Its official establishment is with the signing of the Memorandum of Understanding between UEFA and the ECA on January 21, 2008. The Association of European Clubs has adopted an organizational structure and selection process similar to those on which the Forum of the European Clubs was based, made up of 102 members with a two-year term of office.

open a confrontation with the top representatives of the category, reaching a draft agreement that by March 2021 will become official and will enter into force in view of the summer session of the 2021 football market (Covid-19 permitting).

Throughout 2018, there were several meetings in Zurich and other European locations between the heads of the FIFA committee and representatives of the European Football Agents Association (Efaa), chaired by the Dutchman Rob Jansen. For more than 10 years, this body has represented almost all the national associations of agents in Europe as well as some of the most important in the world such as Argentina, Brazil, and Japan. In Dubai, on January 2 and 3, 2019, a major panel was held as part of Globe Soccer[14] with the participation of Zvone Boban (FIFA vice-secretary), Fabio Paratici (head of the technical area of Juventus FC), and Giovanni Branchini (Efaa vice-president). On this occasion, the importance of the role of agents was reaffirmed not only for the football market, but also for the training of athletes itself. This will result in a new Agents Regulation, which, according to FIFA's[15] official website, will enter into force in the summer of 2020 and will reintroduce the licensing system, centrally administered by FIFA with an enabling examination. In addition, the mandatory liability insurance will be reintroduced, and it will be necessary to update itself through professional courses on an annual basis in order to maintain the license, which can only be granted to natural persons and not to legal entities. Another important innovation that has emerged from the FIFA Executive Board is the inclusion of agents within FIFA TMS[16] (Transfer matching system), the international

---

[14] Ed. "Globe Soccer" is an annual meeting dedicated to the main players in the transfer market, considered as one of the most exclusive events in the sector, where the operators of the transfer market, together with the clubs, leagues, federations, and football institutions can meet and debate. Starting with the second edition of Globe Soccer, the Globe Soccer Awards have been launched, special awards dedicated to the best manager and the best football player's agent of the year.

[15] Also look at www.fifa.com/governance/

[16] What is the TMS, then? The FIFA regulation speaks of an "information and data system on the Internet whose main objective is to simplify the process of international transfer of footballers (male professionals in the field of football for

transfer management system, in which the agent will have to enter each transaction and communicate the information regarding the individual transfer operations concluded. FIFA will pay particular attention to the possibility of conflict of interest; in particular, the prosecutor may be involved in the same transaction only on behalf of the player and the transferee or the transferee club but not all three. In addition, the reform also includes a contribution to the Solidarity Fund by the prosecutors: 5 percent of the sums collected for the sale of footballers to the clubs that raised them will not only be paid by the clubs but also by the agents of the players concerned. Finally, with regard to the dispute settlement system, the agent may alternately use two solutions: resolution through the FIFA and CAS[17] systems and the establishment of the so-called Clearing House, or a transaction settlement system operated by FIFA, which will facilitate the payment of fees. In addition, the system of sanctions, already present in the previous sports system, will be reinserted. The last reform that is to be implemented is the inclusion of a salary cap on salaries paid to prosecutors, but this novelty will have to go beyond the scrutiny of European regulations and consequently of other international confederations. A major problem which, despite the reform, remains to be resolved, concerns the membership of the players' agent. At present, even if the intermediary is not a member, he must be subject to a number of duties placed by the international sporting order without being able to benefit from the rights, such as a more rapid settlement of disputes arising from the non-payment of the fees due to him.

In short, therefore, the reforms that FIFA intends to introduce at the end of 2020 can be summarized as follows:

- RETURN TO THE REGISTER—With the return of the FIFA register, all representatives of the players will have to take an examination and submit to the rules for the category

---

eleven, ed), to improve optimization of information flow." This is a mandatory procedure for transfers: "without the use of the TMS, a purchase is considered null and void."

[17] CAS: Court of arbitration for sport, è il Tribunale arbitrale internazionale dello sport, organismo giudiziario con sede a Losanna, Svizzera.

and periodically attend refresher courses. So, even relatives (such as Wanda Nara, Icardi's wife and *de facto agent*) will have to adapt to these rules in order to have a role.

- PUBLIC COMPENSATION—In the future, compensation for agents will become public, indicating the figures for each individual transaction. On the contrary, clubs now only provide aggregated data that does not allow you to know specifically the extent of relationships with each consultant.
- PAY CAP—The agents have given the willingness to set a ceiling on their compensation if this criterion were also to be applied to other professional figures in football.
- SOLIDARITY FUND—If the compensation ceiling system is introduced, prosecutors will also contribute to the FIFA solidarity fund with which clubs donate 5 percent of the sums collected for the sale of footballers to the companies that raised them.
- CLEARING HOUSE—FIFA will set up a clearing house, which will record all operations and thus be able to monitor relations between clubs, athletes, and agents. This is a fundamental prerequisite for possible measures.
- YOUTH PROSECUTORS—Reformers have also photographed the phenomenon of paying abnormal sums to the families of young footballers. In this respect, it is intended to carry out controls to prevent unscrupulous individuals from "buying" prosecutors at a young age, jeopardizing the careers of grass talents, and exposing them to excessive pressure.

This empirical reconstruction therefore leads to a *return to the past*, that is, to the regulatory regime prior to the FIFA regime of 2015. With this latest reform, there was complete consistency between supranational—the so-called FIFA regulation—and national rules.

The regulatory regime of 2015 had led operators and authors to talk, as mentioned, about deregulation, where conditional access to the profession through enabling examination had been replaced by the mere possession of *minimum standards/requirements*.

In this regulatory system, in fact, access to the profession of sports agent, or rather *intermediary*, was not conditional on passing an enabling examination, as has historically happened, but became in fact free to anyone, subject to requirements of good repute or, in any case, of independence.

On the other hand, the situation that occurs, for example, in Italy, the second nation in the world by volume of commissions paid to sports prosecutors by companies, to date is in close continuity with the previous one, where professionals involved in the negotiation of contracts must, in order to operate, be registered in the appropriate register (or Register) at the Federation, which is accessed following the issue of a license/enabling title.

The same operate within the Sports Order, are required to comply with the relevant regulations and are subject to Sports Justice, but this is not by virtue of an associative bond—the so-called *membership*—as provided for players, clubs, managers, and so on, but on a voluntarist basis with registration in the Register, a prodromic to which there is precisely the acceptance of this systematic-normative corpus.

In the current Italian national football system, therefore, the sports agent could be considered a work provider—a natural or legal person—registered in a professional register with conditional access, which acts under a mandate by assuming a result obligation. A varied figure, as mentioned, not only in terms of domestic law, but also at international-private level, where the hermeneutic effort could lead to the solution (of reasonable compromise) to bring the case back within the scope of the mandate more than other types such as the agency of common law or the provision of services.

In the opinion of the writer, these interpretative considerations, although laudable and, in some ways, essential perhaps take second place if we consider the following assumptions. In the legal transaction concerned, the differences between the elements of one, rather than the other cases of common law, fade, giving rise to a contractual type which is consistent in its practical and consolidated application. Although not typical, the legal transaction in question is known in its elements binding on the subjects of the same operating in the sports system.

Secondly, the mandate of a sports agency and the activity of the football agents—although not typical in the state system, although indirectly recognitions of this kind there are—are certainly *typical*, known—also by the related bodies of justice—in the system in which they express themselves, the federal one, affecting only residually the state procedural system (physiologically civil or tax).

Finally, since the general and peaceful principle of the protection of the autonomy of the parties referred to in Article 10 of the Directive still applies, it is clear from the case-law of the Court of Justice that, in the present case, it is for the National Court to determine whether, in the light of the circumstances of the case, it is necessary to, according to 1322 of the Civil Code, "the parties may also conclude contracts which do not belong to types having special rules, provided that they are dedicated to the rate of interests worthy of protection under the legal system."

Without reaching the hyperbole that the practical and economic application of the case is the driver for legal interpretation, it is still true that in this case, the type of negotiation is ontologically dynamic and susceptible to continuous changes on the basis of concrete experience.

Sports prosecutors in recent years have become crucial in the football market negotiations to say the least. All this because now the various football clubs are called upon to deal not only with the will of the players, but also with multiple and often salty economic commissions.

Consequently, as mentioned above, FIFA is considering introducing a new regulation in order to try to curb the freedom of negotiation of the agents. This is a set of rules that would impose a ceiling on the sums to be paid to managers, among other reforms.

The International Football Federation (FIFA) led by Gianni Infantino aims to impose precise limits. There is talk of the limit between 5 percent and 10 percent of the transfer fees from the company it sells. To this, 3 percent would be added for those who buy and another 3 percent for the player interested in changing jerseys.

Faced with this squeeze, however, the sports prosecutors declared themselves open to dialogue with the institutions of the football field even if still ready to fight in the event of unbalanced contradiction between the parties.

On Monday, January 20, 2019, an important dinner was held in London among the main managers of the football world in which the author of this book also took part with honor.

On this occasion, FIFA's imminent decision to officially limit the commissions relating to player transfers was discussed. The agents have already decided to join, appealing to the freedom of enterprise, endangered by a feared regulatory intervention by FIFA, excessively stringent for an activity, that of the football agents, which in 2020 is decidedly multifaceted, therefore not includable in predetermined hetero-imposed hinges.

Football clubs, federations, and national leagues, on the other hand, are still waiting to decide what to do. On the one hand, they would welcome the new regulation with a sigh of relief.

On the other hand, however, they would not want to get to the head-on confrontation with sports prosecutors. In fact, in the market, they will still be called upon to deal with them. It would therefore not be convenient for relations to be strained and to get to a mutual closure.

In fact, under any circumstances, it is now essential for the clubs to find an agreement with the football agents. Even in the case of zero parameters, if you do not pay the cost of the card to another team, the money must still be paid to the representatives or mediators of the athletes. Always through commissions.

This situation has arisen precisely and especially since 2015, when the so-called deregulation desired by the then FIFA President Joseph Blatter was introduced: that is, the removal of any kind of license or mandate constraint.

In other words, a prosecutor in the course of a negotiation can represent not only the player, but also the company that buys and the one that sells. So, full power and relevant commissions.

And it is no coincidence that in 2019, just considering international affairs, the category has pocketed a total of about 654 million dollars in commissions. That figure has tripled in just five years. And if you look at purchases nationwide, you get to almost a billion dollars.

Relations between agents, on the one hand, and sports clubs and athletes, on the other

Having highlighted the prodromal aspects of access to the profession, we can focus on the concrete contents of this activity.

A subordinate condition for carrying it out is having obtained an assignment in the form of a mandate from the client, sports club or player, as will be seen, sports clubs and/or football players). Formal contract, with mandatory written form, with the additional burden of depositing—by the agent in charge—the mandate with the Federal Agents Commission.

Contract, moreover, subject to nullity in case it is not integrated with the *summary model* (executive summary) available on the Federation website and reporting the essential elements of the store.

Physiologically, the assignment is conferred by one of the parties involved (the company that intends to acquire the federative and economic rights related to the sporting performance of a player; the one that intends to transfer these rights; the club that intends to register an athlete or sign/renew a sports employment contract with a player; a player who must negotiate the first signing or renewal of his employment contract with the employer company).

However, there is no express prohibition of the hypothesis of a joint mandate, even if in clear conflict of interest. The assumption is in fact undisputed: in a multi-party negotiation, the interest of one necessarily affects that of the others. And then, a club that intends to acquire a player, if required to pay a higher sum as remuneration to the latter, will probably negotiate a reduction in the consideration to be paid to the transferring company for said transfer.

Nonetheless, the cases are expressly legitimized and governed by the provision of mechanisms for the prior acceptance of the conflict of interest by the parties in charge, to protect them on the assumption they are informed.

The mandate, then, in the event that it has been conferred by a club for the registration of a player, a different hypothesis, therefore, from the transfer of the same from one company to another, automatically ceases to produce effects when the player in question is no longer registered for the sending club.

In regards to the content, the mandate may provide for an exclusivity in favor of the agent and must expressly provide for the payment deadlines (while the method, by bank transfer, is bound by regulation) and the subjects required to pay the obligation, it may be the case that, for example, the obligation to grant the consideration in favor of the player's agent is not the latter but conventionally the sports club.

Consideration that can be determined in a lump sum or in a percentage calculated on the player's total gross income or the economic values of the transaction.

The so-called temporary football agents. Possible doubts from the point of view of European labor law

As can be easily learned from both national and international regulations, both the state and federal legislators have provided for a transitional regime operating until the end of 2019 (when the new regulation of sports agents in the individual federations came into force national sports), temporarily legitimizing agents in possession of a post March 31, 2015, qualification to operate.

In particular, for this purpose in Italy, Germany, and Portugal, for example, the national sports federation has established the Provisional Federal Register of the so-called Temporary Agents.

The latter, in substance, are subject to the same rules provided for by the discipline of the reform extensively examined in the previous pages.

It then becomes interesting—with ideas that, as will be seen, embrace the principles of EU labor law—to define the Temporary Agent.

In particular, in Italy, the specific Federal Regulation allows the registration in the relevant register to persons who are in possession of a qualification issued by the FIGC between March 31, 2015 and December 31, 2017.

In this regard, there is first of all a question of regulatory consistency: why not allow the exercise of activity in the transitional regime by professionals with a federal qualification after December 31, 2017 (and before the entry into force of the new discipline)?

Secondly and more interestingly, the distance between the trenchant provision for temporary staff—whose qualification was issued, during the relevant period, (exclusively) by the National Sports Federation—and that of the ordinary post-reform discipline, which, as seen, provides for wide dissertation on the possibilities of access to the profession granted to Community agents, is immediately a source of attention.

Taking a concrete example, a Spanish agent, authorized by his National Federation after March 31, 2015 and before December 31, 2017, could not operate in Italy, even until December 31, 2019 (except in the case of passing the examination of the new regime), with all the consequent findings in terms of Euro-unitary labor law regarding possible contrasts with the cardinal principles of supranational fundamental freedoms, including, first of all, the freedom to provide services. As it is known, the rules of the European Treaties provide—and indeed it is the pillar of the common market—for the right to exercise freely, on a temporary and occasional basis, its service activities in the Member State where the service is provided, under the same conditions as those imposed by that State on its own nationals, with the consequent prohibition of restrictions on that freedom to provide services.

If the rationale of the ordinary scheme is considered reasonable, which, moreover, applies to both Italian and Community agents, which only saves the qualifications issued before March 31, 2015 (before the so-called deregulation), the basis of a derogation from the requirement that applies only to professionals, for example, Italian and not to Community professionals are not easily understood.

In this respect, it should be pointed out that the prohibited restrictions are not only direct restrictions—for example, based on the mere fact of the nationality of the provider—but also indirect restrictions, such as those that could be found in state and FIGC regulations.

Restrictions which, moreover, in the economic sector concerned, that of professional football, are all the more striking when we consider that *social dumping*[18] is ontologically absent because of the inherent characteristics of the activity and its market-driven profitability.

It is a system of rules that have been positive on the basis of the guidelines formed and consolidated by the case law of the Court of Justice of the European Union in a process of integration of the services market and in the wake of the 10-year pro-labor policies. From this point of view, there is also the question of possible restrictions on the access to the profession, which, as we have seen, are the most incisive elements of the legislative and endo-federal reform that has just been

---

[18] Social dumping: An expression used to indicate the practice of some companies (especially multinationals) of locating their business in areas where they can benefit from less restrictive labor provisions or where labor costs are lower. In this way, the lower costs for the company can be transferred to the final price of the asset that is more competitive.

examined. Are national provisions that make the pursuit of a professional activity in a Member State subordinate the pursuit of certain require-ments, the passing of particular examinations, or a minimum period of experience compatible with the libertarian principles of European law? These forecasts, although justified by an objective rationale, could intro-duce obstacles to the free movement of professionals and could therefore be anti-competitive. An answer to this question is not possible here. The institute's well-established historicity—before the aforementioned dereg-ulation, both the FIFA regulation and those of the national federations, provided for the enabling examination for the exercise of the activity of sports prosecutor—never called into question by the European Justice System, and the probable proportionality of the examination test with respect to the relevant interests and with a view to the general balance of the same, would in any case lead to an affirmative solution regarding the lawfulness of such rules.

Conclusions

Adhering to metaphors on the subject of treatment, the *chronicle* set out in the previous pages tells of a competition played by the team of opera-tors in the sector—clubs, footballers, agents, and professionals—away on the field of the national and sports legislator, which ended drawing up an initial assessment after the first concrete application of the legislative reform, with an honorable tie.

As seen, I do not take into account the difficulties encountered by the interested parties in comparing with the new regulatory system, between new obligations and vetoes on access to the profession of not immediate solution.

Nevertheless, it must be admitted that any new discipline, all the more so within the perimeter of the sporting order, in which rules of different levels, state, and internal, live with each other, bring with it physiological transitional difficulties.

There is no doubt that the principles that inspired the reform seem to be acceptable. A return to professionalization of the activity, allowed only to qualified subjects, is legitimate given the well-known position rents that permeate the intermediates related to the transfers of players between clubs.

The complexities (and the above doubts in point of law) have arisen with regard to certain choices—it can be said, for excludendum—made by the legislator tracing regime dystonia between certain subjects and others. In particular, between the agents qualified before March 31, 2015, and those in possession of a license issued subsequently; and again, between those Italian agents and those on other Community agents authorized or not to operate temporarily under transitional regime until the end of the year 2019.

As mentioned above, here is what FIFA posted on its website[19] on January 22, 2020, regarding the figure of the new sports agents.

The Football Stakeholders Committee and the FIFA Council unanimously endorsed last year a series of reform proposals concerning football agents with the aim to protect the integrity of football and prevent abuses. These measures were the result of an extensive consultation process with stakeholders (players, clubs, leagues, and member associations), as well as agents who were invited to several consultation meetings.

The overarching objective here is to improve transparency, protect player welfare, enhance contractual stability, and also raise professional and ethical standards. In other words, to eliminate or at least reduce the abusive and excessive practices, which unfortunately have existed in football.

FIFA, as football's governing body, has the responsibility to address and regulate these matters. We are aiming for a system of balanced and reasonable regulation, instead of the law of the jungle currently in place, with conflicts of interests rife and exorbitant *commissions* being earned left and right.

In the last year alone, football agents earned USD 653.9 million in fees, four times more than in 2015.

The reform package therefore includes several measures concerning agents:

- Establishment of a cap on commissions to avoid excessive and abusive practices

---

[19] Please refer to the official FIFA website for the full text: https://fifa.com/who-we-are/news/reform-proposals-concerning-football-agents-regulations

- Limitation of multiple representation to avoid conflicts of interest
- Reintroduction of a mandatory licensing system for agents to raise professional standards
- Creation of a FIFA Clearing House to guarantee better financial transparency
- Establishment of an effective FIFA dispute resolution system to address disputes between agents, players, and clubs
- Disclosing and publishing all agent-related work in transfers, to increase transparency, improve the credibility of the transfer system, and support the implementation of new regulations

All these proposals from FIFA on agent regulation are sensible, reasonable, rational, proportionate, and necessary to protect the interests of players and the wider interests of football. They are also in line with sentiment repeatedly expressed by institutions such as the European Commission and European Parliament.

FIFA is currently developing these proposals to be turned into regulations. Once again, this work is done in consultation with the football stakeholders, including agents' representatives.

> If we asked people in the street what they thought of intermediaries I'm sure critics would label them money grabbers or blame them for the hyper-inflation of transfer prices. By contrast, supporters might argue that intermediaries constitute an essential part of the football ecosystem. What neither would really discuss is whether FIFA should regulate this group or not, but it's a key consideration for FIFA at the moment

says Santiago Barroso Torres in his article.[20]

In order to understand the context of the oncoming reform in the way intermediaries are regulated, we have to cast our minds back to the

---

[20] See: https://lexsportiva.blog/tag/dual-representation/

FIFA Players Agents Regulations issued in 2008. FIFA Players Agents Regulations were a complex system of regulations based on the concept of an *agent* as a person who, for a fee, negotiates employment contracts to conclude transfer agreements.

Under the Agents Regulations system, it was actually very difficult to become an agent; you had to be licensed by the relevant association. When qualified, you could only represent one party in a negotiation and any international disputes where agents were involved would be settled by the FIFA Players Status Committee.

After a few years of the complex regulations, FIFA realized that their system was not up to par and did not meet their expectations. Some deficits that FIFA identified were that:

1. Only 25 to 30 percent of acting agents actually had a license.
2. Agents and clubs preferred not to report transactions in which they participated.
3. There were many discrepancies between national regulations regarding the activities of agents.

Due to these failings, FIFA issued the Regulations on Working with Intermediaries in April 2015 and this is the regulatory system that operates today.

Unlike the previous regime, this system is based in the concept of an *intermediary* as a natural or legal person who, for a fee or free of charge, represents players and/or clubs in order to conclude an employment contract or represents clubs in negotiations to conclude transfer agreements. In contravention with the FIFA Players Agents Regulations 2008, FIFA decided to deregulate Agents. This meant that the intermediaries no longer needed a license in order to provide services. In fact, any person regardless of their expertise could be involved in a player's transfer, for example. Other relevant changes were that intermediaries were able to represent a player and a club. This meant that dual representation was permitted as long as both the club and the player consented in writing and prior to the start of the negotiations and established which party shall remunerate the intermediary. Furthermore, since intermediaries were out of the football ecosystem, the Player's Status Committee (or any other FIFA dispute resolution body) no longer had jurisdiction on matters relating to intermediaries.

Yet again, FIFA found that such a system of regulations didn't achieve the desired objectives that they were looking for. During a conference by Emilio García Silvero (Chief Legal Officer, FIFA) entitled "Towards a new Regulatory Framework for the Transfers of Football Players: Evolution or Revolution?" held at the "Instituto Superior de Derecho y Economía (ISDE)," he mentioned:

"It was a mistake to de-regulate agents in 2015."

Today, it seems as if regulation is back in fashion and he hinted that important changes will be introduced including a licensing system administered centrally by FIFA through a web-based examination, which an aspiring intermediary will be required to pass in order to practice. The aim of this was to ensure integrity and regain trust in the profession. Bringing intermediaries back into the fold also affords them access to the effective and efficient dispute resolution systems of FIFA/CAS. FIFA also intended to create a "clearing house" through which all payments to intermediaries will be registered in order to better understand and regulate the way intermediaries are paid. There will also be guidelines that prohibit conflicts of interest in dual representation cases. For example, representing:

- Player + Engaging Club = allowed
- Player + Releasing Club = prohibited
- Releasing Club + Engaging club = prohibited

In relation to the famous recommended pay cap for services, it is important to mention that apparently such remuneration would not be limited, as long as all the parties are aware of the payments made to the intermediaries. This increases transparency as all parties must be aware of all different steps undertaken within negotiations, including the agent's fees and any payments directly or indirectly related to the player. Finally, there will be a sanctioning system in place to deal with non-compliant clubs, players, and intermediaries.

CHAPTER 2

Comparative Examination of the Figure of the Football Agent in the European "Big Five Sisters" and Its Historical Excursus

From the dawn of the profession to today, the football agent has seen a radical evolution of this professional figure, passing from working alone to an increasingly frequent associative form. Increasingly, agents have been associated under one big shield, one multinational company capable of including various customers for their most various needs.

The excellent study carried out by Raffaele Poli, professor and researcher of the CIES Football Observatory, of the University of Neuchâtel, Professor Giambattista Rossi, of Birkbec University of London, and Dr. Roger Besson, also from CIES Football Observatory, published by Routledge Taylor & Francis in the book "Sports Agents and Labor Markets" highlights how the legal framework at the head of FIFA of this figure, which today we define professional for membership more or less generalized of the same to a professional register or at least to a register, is actually one very recent news, given that it is only since 1991 that FIFA has decided to establish the first register of FIFA agents posted on their official website.

Ten years later, in November 2011, there were 6,082 agent licenses worldwide: About 40 percent are domiciled in the Big Five sisters: England, Spain, Germany, Italy, and France. The illustrious work just mentioned, first of all studies the market shares of players' representation in the five most important European leagues. By presenting the results of a survey questionnaire, it analyzes the socio-demographic profile of licensed football agents, analyzes their corporate sector and the diversification of services offered by individual agencies. From the following study, it is possible to derive some indicative factors of a trend that has now crystallized in the market, namely that the Big Five sisters and their transfers strongly influence the rest of the global transfer market. The study in the analysis reveals the existence of closed relational networks that clearly favor the concentration of players under the control of a few agents.

Only 3.4 percent of the sample is female, which confirms that until today, the activity of football agents is still almost completely male centered.

Another interesting data is certainly given by the personal data, in fact the average age of the agents in the reference sample is 42 years. Two-thirds of them are included in the age group of 31 to 50 years.

Interestingly, a quarter of them operated for the first time without a regular license. This shows that authorized agents are clearly not the only intermediaries involved in the conclusion of a transfer transaction, but we will discuss this in more detail in Chapter 5 when we will address the difficult issue of management in relations with the families of players. More than half of the respondents (54%) were already part of the football world before becoming an agent. This activity, as we will recall several times, is strongly characterized by personal relationships, so it is clear that those who have a substantial past as a footballer could have an advantage in taking the first steps in the world of football intermediation; the first steps indeed. Because, mind you, having a past as a footballer can be a favorable condition but certainly not sufficient to become a good sports agent. Indeed, it is certainly no coincidence that no former famous footballer has become a popular agent.

In terms of the business structure through which agents operate, the survey questionnaire reveals that a small majority of the study's respondents (51%) have established their own agency. Only half of the companies founded by agents have shareholders other than the founder, also complicit in federal endo regulations which, upon registering their sports agency, try to put professionals who do not have any sporting qualification out of the federal world. Of these companies, nearly 70 percent have no more than two shareholders. In nearly eight out of ten cases, the authorized agent is the main shareholder.

Another data that will certainly be useful to us, and that will be analyzed more deeply in the last chapter, is that related to the type of services rendered by the agent. While negotiating is the most frequent service provided (98% of the sample analyzed), almost two-thirds of them also assist their clients with marketing and specialization contracts while also providing some sort of legal advice and dispute resolution. Surprisingly, only a minority of agents (46%) support their clients in personal care activities such as finding a home or apartment, organizing travel, helping family members, and so on. This result shows that the general view of agents as 360° *protectors* of their clients does not correspond to reality.

A different reading from the prevailing opinion that I feel I can provide is the one about the *bad reputation* of football agents, who, according to the majority press, are interested in having their client transferred whenever the opportunity arises, to make money on the new professional contract stipulated. The need for many agents to negotiate short-term deals is often found in the well-defined willingness of clubs to sign contracts for professionals, for one, maximum two years. This professional investment mentality of some clubs, in the *short term*, is detrimental to the career prospects of young players who will be aware of having to fight hard to get a reconfirmation the following year and, consequently, of agents intent already at six months from the natural expiry of the contract, to ideally seek new solutions. In order to develop their business, the authorized agents work closely with other professionals. Sporting directors, technical directors, coaches, and presidents are clearly indicated as the most important professional partners when negotiating an employment contract between agents and clubs. Almost 40 percent of the agents interviewed by the aforementioned research have already represented at least one football manager. The large percentage of agents who manage the careers of players and coaches at the same time has often caused the problem raised by the federations and the sports justice bodies, regarding the legitimacy of this activity as regards the aspect of conflicts of interest (even if only potential) between an agent who represents a player who, for different dynamics, finds himself playing in the club coached by the coach, who in turn is also represented by the same agent. This potential conflict of interest, in my humble opinion, is made even more acute, if you want, by the infamous Blatter reform of 2015, which in fact placed the activity of football agents (now intermediaries for FIFA) in the middle between the two figures since they could represent professionals, footballer, and club. The very high risk of conflicts of interest on the part of the football agent is evident. From this worrying perspective, the English Premier League's decision to make public the figures of the commissions paid by clubs to agents generated. Furthermore, in 2011, FIFA expressed in favor of the hypothesis of publication of the remuneration paid to intermediaries, so much so that in the aforementioned reform project launched by FIFA in 2018, which will see its conclusion toward the first months of 2021, due to a slowdown in the work caused by the global pandemic from Covid-19, an important obligation of transparency has been provided for the football clubs that use the professional activity of a sports agent in the negotiation of an employment contract for a football player, which takes the form of obligation on the part of the companies to publish the data related to the commissions paid to agents for each individual transaction, and no longer, as in use until last year, to simply publish the more generic aggregate data.

FIFA has also provided for the obligation to register online on the platform developed for international transfers (Transfer Matching System) of sports agents. Based on the data from the UEFA comparison report, we can estimate that the annual turnover of football agents in UEFA-affiliated national associations is around 400 million euros, exactly double that estimated for all the sports agents in the EU in 2008 by a study launched by the European Commission. In 2015, the five major European leagues generated total revenues of €11.3 billion and spent €6.7 billion in wage costs and transfer taxes (Deloitte, 2015). Measuring the turnover of intermediaries has always been a difficult task. The English leagues have led the way in terms of transparency, with the FA (English Football Association) reporting annually on the fees that clubs pay to agents.

Given the international nature of the sector, various other reports have tried to demonstrate the size of the "agent market" across Europe: in 2014, the European Court published a study on the player transfer system, based on the previous work by the European Commission and stated that, during the 2011/2012 and 2012/2013 football seasons, UEFA clubs spent $254 million on club agent fees, equivalent to 14.6 percent of the total value of the transfers in the same clubs. Unsurprisingly, clubs in

Europe's top leagues have pledged to pay the highest commissions to agents, totaling $197 million, practically 80 percent of the total.

Since October 2010, TMS FIFA has tracked all the international transfers in football and its "Global Transfer Report" states that between 2011 and 2014, $754 million was spent by clubs paying commissions to intermediaries for their roles in international transfers.

These exorbitant figures must not make you turn up your nose. The figure of the football agent is essential in the successful conclusion of a transfer. The agent is often a friend or a trusted man of footballers and their families, he knows the dynamics within the decision-making process of his client and, basically, he knows when to sink the shot and when to refuse. It is the first true ally of the clubs. Returning then to the calculations from the TMS, also published by Deloitte in the same year, suggest that agents received about 6 percent of the commissions for each transfer and that transfer costs are increasing from year to year, so much so that it is estimated that commissions will double at the end of 2020.[1]

The analysis borrowed, as regards to the statistical and methodological part by G. Rossi, A. Semens, and J.F. Brocard in their Sports Agents and Labor Markets text, provides us with an important basis on which to develop our comparative study that will highlight the main differences between the five most important European national sports federations, with regard to the figure of the football agent.

These five are defined in common football jargon as the "Big Five sisters" and alone move most of the world's affairs. That is, they are capable of influencing the football world by themselves.

The Market for Agent and Intermediaries in England

The England of hooligans and empty stadiums, besieged by the police of M. Thatcher who harshly condemned those weekend acts of violence, ended in 1992. The year in which the Premier League actually entered the field. Currently, England is the most attractive and profitable league for players and, consequently, for their agents.

---

[1] Cfr. https://fifatms.com/data-reports/reports/ 2015

English Premier League[2] has adopted strict rules to govern the activities of agents, in particular by demanding transparency in transfers after two major "bung scandals."[3] The FA's first investigation began in 1995 in response to allegations of illegal payments made in a British High Court case between Terry Venables and Alan Sugar, surrounding Teddy Sheringham's transfer from Nottingham Forest to Tottenham Hotspur. The FA's investigation lasted three and a half years and considered several domestic and international transfers between 1992 and 1994. In September 1997, the investigative report revealed the increasing influence agents had on financial transactions and revealed a lack of financial strength within English football.

A practice, that of tax evasion, which unfortunately constantly proliferates. The story of a few years ago is sadly known, in which Sam Allardyce, Massimo Cellino, and JF Hasselbaink (the latter later cleared and defended by the QPR, the club he coached at the time) ended up in a media fuss for alleged rounds of illegal money. This sad story is the last in chronological order, but betting and infiltration of the underworld continue and will continue to enter football if the justice bodies of the ball do not enter the disciplinary level also on the criminal side.

However, there was no real political will on the part of the football universe to acknowledge the problem and discipline tougher punishments, such as a lifetime ban (and not with a single year of inhibition from the world of football). In other words, football authorities did not try hard enough to ensure that multimillion-dollar transfers conformed to their rules. Already in the past, the English FA has tried to intervene with 39 recommendations[4] to make significant changes and improve transparency, as well as give the governing body greater regulatory control over the business of those involved in the transfer market.

---

[2] The Premier League, also known as the English Premier League (EPL) outside of England, is the top flight of the English football league. The Premier was born in 1992, after the 22 teams affiliated to the First Division (the then top English league) decided to leave the Football League for economic reasons.

[3] Cfr. The indipendent.co.uk, "Top managers identified in 'bung' scandal" By Sam Wallace Tuesday, September 19, 2006.

[4] Cfr. http://thefa.com/football-rules-governance/lawsandrules

Major reforms included a ban on double representation, a requirement for overseas agents to register with the FA when involved in a move to England, and the need to disclose the total amount of agent fees paid by clubs each year. In 2007, the FA also established a monitoring group that oversees and analyzes the player transfer market and payments to football agents made through the *clearing house* system, which collects transfer transaction data and is organized in partnership between PL and FL. The FA (Football Association) is responsible for monitoring and paying the commissions paid to agents who are also integrated into the clearing system. In December 2007, the FA worked closely with law enforcement authorities and developed a comprehensive guide to football clubs on money laundering with a dedicated law on false accounting and bankruptcy offences fraudulent. While all these measures provide only partial solutions, the UK transfer market is now considered to be one of the most transparent and rigorous, where agents are deemed to be promptly and reasonably remunerated compared to the other European transfer markets.

This reputation was confirmed when the PL (Premier League) decided to ban TPOs[5] from the beginning of the 2008/09 season. In this historical

---

[5] TPO: (Third Party Ownership): See www.diritto.it, the TPO agreements in professional football. "Third-party ownership (TPO) agreement is a type of investment that third parties, not part of the sports system (e.g., investment funds, private entities), make by acquiring all or part of the economic rights of professional sportsmen, in order to profit from any future transfers of such athletes. These practices appear to be widespread especially in football. The rapid spread and not always transparent use of TPOs has been discussed at various levels within the international football community. FIFA coordinated the discussions on an international level, which took place in various standing FIFA committees, such as the Football Committee, the Committee for Club Football and the Players' Status Committee. A working group was therefore created with the aim of further studying the phenomenon of OPT. Various football organizations in the world have come to prohibit TPOs (FIFA, but also the FA Premier League), considering these practices a threat to the integrity of competitions, to the development of young players and to the too strict and not very transparent constraint establishes between the players and the third party owner of the card. In the FIFA headquarters, Circular 1464/2014 was published in which FIFA communicated to the various national football federations associated with it that

context, where British football was struggling to find a regulatory framework capable of framing the figure of agents, now intermediaries, FIFA

---

the Regulations on the Status and Transfer of Players (RSTP - Regulations on the Status and Transfer of Players) would be amended to include new provisions on TPO and players' economic rights (Article 18 ter) for which no club or player may enter into agreements with third parties for which the third party may receive compensation for the transfer of a player from a club to another, or to enter into agreements for which the third party may be the beneficiary of an economic right on the future transfer of a player. The TPO ban entered into force on 1 May 2015. The new provisions are binding and must be included without modification in the regulations of the national football associations associated with FIFA. Previously, in the RSTP Regulations, a rule had been inserted concerning the relations between Third-party and football clubs, in order to exclude any type of interference by the Third-party on corporate decisions. Article 18 bis of the Regulations on the Status and Transfers of FIFA Players provides that 'no company may enter into contracts that allow any other party included in the contract or third parties to acquire the ability to influence employment relationships and on issues relating to transfers, his autonomy over political choices or the activity of his own team.' In March 2016, four different professional clubs, Santos Futebol Clube (Brazil), Sevilla FC (Spain), Club K St Truidense VV (Belgium), and FC Twente (Netherlands), were sanctioned by FIFA for having violated the articles 18 bis and 18 ter of the FIFA Regulations on the Status and Transfers of Players. Recently, in March 2017, the TAS (Court of Arbitration for Sport) based in Lausanne issued a very important ruling on the subject of TPO. The CAS rejected the appeal of the Belgian football club FC Seraing recognizing the legitimacy of the prohibition on Third-party ownership (TPO) provided by FIFA in the Regulations on the Status and Transfers of Players, as this prohibition is perfectly compatible with the rules Community in the field of competition. Previously with regard to the specific case, in September 2015, the FIFA Disciplinary Commission had condemned the Belgian second division club FC Seraing with the blockade of the market and a fine of 150 thousand Swiss francs for violating the Regulations on Status and Transfers of the Players on the prohibition of TPO.

The Belgian club for FIFA would have transferred part of the economic rights of several players to a third party, having signed contracts that allowed it to influence the decisions and independence of the club in matters of transfers. The decision of the FIFA Disciplinary Commission was confirmed later in 2016 by the Court of Appeal, rejecting the reasons presented on appeal by the Belgian club. The issue of the TPO was also the subject of debate in the European Parliament. On found fertile ground when it decided to introduce the 2015 regulation on intermediaries. Several *vacatio legis* left room for new rules and extensive interpretations of the same.

Articles 1.2 and 1.3 of the FIFA Regulations on working with Intermediaries of April 1, 2015, while requiring the individual national sports federations to implement and reinforce the provisions coming from Zurich, expressly reserves the *right* to "Go beyond these minimum standards/requirements." In February 2015, the FA, aware of how little has been done until then, was one of the first federations to publish its own supplementary internal regulation, called "the FA Regulation on Working with Intermediaries." In England, to date, the matter that regulates the activity of the intermediary (the FA intermediary) can be divided into three independent sources but which interact with each other:

UK legislation: Although there is no specific sector regulation that directly regulates the activity of football intermediaries, there are nevertheless a number of statutes that directly impact the conduct or the freedom to act of the most generic intermediaries. "The Bribery Act" of 2010

November 11, 2015, the European Parliament presented a 'Written declaration, submitted pursuant to article 136 of the regulation, on the prohibition of the ownership of third parties on the cards of players in European sport' with which it strongly condemns the ownership by third party investors of a sports card. The reasons for this Declaration are manifold in nature. The Declaration notes, first of all, that this type of agreement represents a practice contrary to one of the cardinal principles of the European Union, namely respect for human dignity (Article 2 of the Treaty on European Union): in the specific case The European Union aims to effectively address human trafficking and also to guarantee the integrity of professional sportspeople. Secondly, this type of contract represents a strong limitation for professional athletes, some of them very young, who cannot freely choose their professional career as their card is owned by third party/private investors. Finally, the European Union affirms that Third-party ownerships represent a real danger to the validity of sports competitions. These practices are often not very transparent and are fertile ground for criminal activities of various kinds, from the manipulation of sports scores to money laundering. The debate on Third-party ownership still appears to be extremely important and topical given that this type of mechanism is still widespread in South America where European football clubs are looking for new talent and new business."

is a relevant legislation that all intermediaries, without distinction, must bear in mind given that this legislation establishes two *criminal offences*:

(1)   Bribing another person[6]

(2)   Being bribed

Instead, it is provided for in paragraph 4 of the Bribery Act that

[I]mproper performance is performance or non-performance which breaches expectations of good faith or impartiality or breaches a position of trust. The penalties under s.11 of the Bribery act are potentially serious: an unlimited fine or imprisonment for up to 10 years.

Most agencies in the UK, especially the most powerful in terms of clients, will also have to pay attention to the provisions of paragraph 7 of the Bribery Act, which states that a commercial organization will itself be found guilty if an *associated person* including an intermediary hired by the organization, *bribes* another person with the intent of obtaining a business advantage for the organization.

Other relevant regulatory acts that emanate directly from UK legislation are the Fraud Act of 2006, the Conduct of Employment Agencies and Employment Business Regulations of 2003 and the Employment Agencies Act of 1973, all united by setting minimum standards of ethical conduct and professional respect, which essentially follows the FIFA regulation on intermediaries of 2015.

The common law: the definition of the agency from the common law is

[T]he fiduciary relationship which exists between two persons one of whom expressly or impliedly manifest assent that the other should act on his behalf so as to affect his relations with third parties, and the other of whom similarly manifests assent so to act or so acts pursuant to the manifestation.[7]

---

[6] Bribery Act 2010 s.1.

[7] Bowstead, B., and F.M.B. Reynolds. 2010. *Bowstead & Reynolds on Agency*, 19th ed, UK, Sweet and Maxwell.

The common law duties that an intermediary must comply with in the performance of its profession include, not exhaustively, the duty to use skill and care, to act in accordance with the legal terms and not to act in a conflict of interest.

The 2015 FIFA Regulations on working with Intermediaries: The assumption from which FIFA had started deciding the deregulation of the agents, which it created itself, was that the FIFA licensing system for agents, which in reality had to be used to catalog and therefore control the work of the same, in reality it turned out immediately not exhaustive. In fact, only 25 to 30 percent of market transactions were officially concluded by internationally licensed agents.[8]

However, this was not the case in England. Over the years, the FA has promulgated a considerable number of rules governing the activity of football agents operating in England, arousing general consensus among all British Football Stakeholders. The regulatory shield raised by the FA is so strong that it is important to emphasize that the FA Regulation expressly states that in the event of a conflict between the FA's internal regulations and the FIFA regulations, federal regulations have the upper hand. This supremacy of national laws over FIFA ones is also and above all important for intermediaries who are external to the FA who want to operate in the UK who must expressly accept federal internal regulations, as well as of course the generic FIFA regulations.

Finally, for those who do not comply with federal legislation, there is the possibility of being sanctioned by the FA, and disputes between two intermediaries, or between intermediaries and players/clubs will be resolved by a federal arbitral tribunal of the FA as the "Rule K of the FA's Rules of the Association."

The Market for Agents and Intermediaries in Italy

The transfer market in Italy is unique considering that it happens in real-time and as such has always been followed by media, fans, and professionals. The event is organized by the Italian Football Federation, the

---

[8] FIFA Director of legal Affairs Marco Villiger "FIFA actss to protect core values" fifa.com, July 15, 2009.

FIGC, in collaboration with the professional leagues and consists of a real "physical" football market in which agents, players, football directors, and club owners meet in a hotel to arrange the transfers during the winter and summer transfer windows. Normally this so-called *spectacularized* market is held twice a year, in three days of events in Milan, the city strategically chosen as the location of the transfer market, because it is well connected to airport networks for international connections. Both in the summer and in the winter, the best hotels in the city center, in turn, compete for the organization of the transfer market event, which obviously brings millions of viewers to follow the latest purchases live on national television networks of this or that company. Several supporters crowd the common areas of the hotel, also accessible to journalists, where we agents, sports directors, football players, and presidents struggle between the floors of the hotel. Each club gets a room, a suite. In order to negotiate a transfer, the agent often has to go directly to a *gallant transfer market match*. The culmination of the event is certainly marked by the clock countdown that marks the end of market operations for that session. All the contracts deposited after that time will not be considered valid. I still remember when Inter managed to buy David Suazo, a player then in force at Cagliari, by blowing him to Milan, literally throwing the contract into the *basket* of contracts, from outside the secretariat's door. The Inter secretary and the agent in question were praised for their sporting skills as well as for having really concluded the operation at the last second. Historically, Italy is recognized as "the most South American nation in Europe," the one that lives on football seven days a week. As a result, the country with the largest number of licensed agents in the world is precisely Italy with almost 1,000 agents. Until the early 2000s, these high numbers of participants also corresponded to the highest parcels. The best commissions were in Italy, and it was always said that if you wanted to be someone in the world of football, your footballer had to come and play in Italy. Unfortunately, a series of scandals, Calciopoli above all, where Juventus was relegated to Serie B, and Milan together with other clubs, heavily penalized for match-fixing, have destroyed the image of Italian football in the media, which took more than 10 years to again attract world champions of the caliber of Cristiano Ronaldo, now registered with Juventus, or Romelu Lukaku, currently in force at Inter. Famous is the phrase of Mourinho, in 2010, the year in which as a coach, he won the treble with Inter, when a journalist had invited him to have a more relaxed attitude in the race for the championship, precisely against Juventus:

> Should we tone down? Let's lower the tone … that's how you Italians build a story that made me a terrible shame as a football professional, as a person who earns from football. I was working in Portugal at the time, but when I learned about Calciopoli it made me ashamed to feed my family with football money. But now … let's tone it down. And I'll tell you another thing: I arrived in Italy an honest man, I will leave Italy a honest man.

This heavy, harsh statement by the *neroazzurro* coach immediately photographed the idea that Italy had given of all the Italian football. The Calciopoli scandal also affected football agents, as it revealed the dominant position of the GEA World agency[9] in the Italian transfer market with an average market share of 10.2 percent from 2002 to 2006 and its representation of players whose transfer values equaled 18.9 percent of the entire market: double the second-largest agency, PDP according to the AGCM[10] report, dated 2006. Recognizing that the football industry

---

[9] The GEA World Agency was founded by Alessandro Moggi son of the then Juventus manager Luciano Moggi, at the center of the Juventus corruption scandal in 2006. This clear connection between father and son signaled to Italian football the clear existence of a serious situation of conflicts of interest within the Italian transfer market system.

[10] Cfr. Antitrust definition (AGCM), Treccani: "Antitrust (Competition and Market Authority, AGCM) Public institution responsible for the protection of competition in the Italian national law. Created by the l. 287/1990 (Rules for the protection of competition and the market), of explicit EU inspiration, has the function of guaranteeing the correct functioning of the market so that economic operators are allowed to access it freely and compete with equal opportunities. Underlying the discipline that the authority is delegated to apply is the idea that, in a free market system, free competition (value directly attributable to articles 41 and 117 of the Constitution): promotes innovation, cost reduction and the qualitative improvement of products; favors the differentiation of products, enriching the alternatives available to consumers; urges inefficient companies to innovate, under penalty of exclusion from the market; prevents an excessive concentration of economic power, setting the conditions for access and affirmation of the most deserving operators. In this way, the efficiency of the economic system and the well-being of consumers are guaranteed."

was completely corrupt, in February 2007 the FIGC introduced an already mentioned new agent regulation. Reform guidelines have been adopted with the aim of widening access to the profession and controls have been put in place to prevent the establishment and abuse of a dominant position on the market by a small group of prosecutors, as was the case with the GEA. More specifically, controls have been implemented in the following areas: (1) integrity of persons admitted to the profession of football agents, (2) standardization of contractual relations between agents and players. The reform focused primarily on combating establishment and subsequent abuse of dominant positions by agents, introducing numerous prohibitions and regulatory incompatibilities to prevent potential conflicts of interest. These included specific clauses relating to the presence of family ties and the number of clubs and players represented by the same group. Paradoxically, the restrictions on the practice of the footballing agent have increased. Provisions aimed at preventing conflicts of interest, in particular, ended up effectively hindering entrepreneurial activity, reducing the freedom of choice of players and clubs and creating obstacles to the competitive development of agents' businesses.

Among the first Italian agencies, PDP was probably the first to transfer Italian players abroad, starting with the transfer of Gianluca Vialli to Chelsea. Funded and managed by veteran agent and lawyer Claudio Pasqualin, its client list includes 184 players such as Sebastian Giovinco, Domenico Criscito, Alberto Aquilani, and Salvatore Bocchetti. The lawyer Giuseppe Bozzo, former collaborator of the PDP agency for the Southern Italy market, has also become a leading agent, creating AGB Sport Management. He began his career assisting Antonio Cassano as a client, from the Bari Calcio youth sector and has grown to become one of the most influential agents, earning an international reputation. His portfolio is worth €67 million and includes players Fabio Quagliarella, Federico Peluso, and Leandro Greco. He was actively involved as a club agent in the transfer of Martin Caceres and Alvaro Morata to Juventus and Mateo Kovacic to Inter.

Personally, I got to know the lawyer Bozzo, through my previous dominus, the lawyer Franco Campana of the "Football Leaders," who among others had collaborated with champions such as Franz Beckenbauer. Two professionals with a capital "P."

Ten years after the GEA World case, the market representation of agents has become increasingly competitive and it is possible to see that the series of reforms introduced with the subsequent agent regulations have had a positive impact on the level of competitiveness among the football representative agencies. Undoubtedly, the market is strongly linked to the current condition of Italian football, which has partly lost its attraction. In this context, Italian agencies are expanding their business in emerging markets such as the United States and Asia.

For years, Italian managers have denounced state aid to Spanish clubs, beneficiaries of the so-called Beckham Law, which we will discuss in the next paragraph, and which lowered taxes on the paychecks of foreign players. With the 2019 Growth decree, a Beckham Law was also effectively enacted for Italian football. And the roles have been reversed, with La Liga president Javier Tebas saying, with an exaggeration, that "in Italy, players pay 10 times less taxes than in Spain" and the newspaper "El pais" entitled "Calcio es un paraiso fiscal"—the italian football is a tax haven.

And they are right.

"The new law is a bomb," summarize in chorus Antonio Tomassini and Antonio Longo, expert lawyers in tax and sports matters of the international law firm DLA Piper. But what exactly is this *bomb*? We are talking about the law converting the Growth Decree which, among the various stimulus measures, has dedicated a chapter to the return of brains by introducing specific tax breaks for professional sportsmen (therefore athletes, coaches, technical-sports directors, and athletic trainers) who have worked abroad in the last two years and transfer their residence to Italy falling within the notion of *repatriated* workers, be they Italians or foreigners. For them, the taxation for Irpef purposes is applied only on 50 percent of the taxable income produced: in essence, they will pay taxes only on half of their income. In truth, the measure is even more advantageous for other workers, taxed only on 30 percent of income. But in the end, Parliament decided not to reward the subjects of a golden world such as football to such an extent, also providing a sort of solidarity contribution, equal to 0.5 percent of the tax base, intended for the strengthening of the youth sectors. Peanuts compared to the savings obtained.

The fact is that consequently to the application of this decree, and also the result of new wealthy foreign presidencies in recent years, for the richest clubs (FC Internazionale is owned by the Suning group, Fiorentina owned by the Italian-American Rocco Commisso, Dan Friedkin, another American for the Roman capital, AS Roma side), Italian football is back, a phenomenon on the rise so as to return to having dedicated thematic channels even across the Channel, with the task of broadcasting C. Ronaldo & Co.

The Market of Agents and Intermediaries in Spain

The transfer market in Spain is decidedly polarized toward a combination of clubs, Real Madrid and Barcelona rarely interspersed with the presence of a third *inconvenience*, often Atletico Madrid or Sevilla. Historically, the Spanish league, except for these two top clubs, does not boast other internationally appreciated realities such as England and Italy. Here, the Spanish government has deemed it appropriate to give a boost to the football sector, with the establishment of ad hoc legislation rewritten to facilitate the purchase of talent from abroad—the so-called Ley Beckham,[11] passed in 2005 and operational until 2010 until its

---

[11] The Lay Beckham: "from" Fisco e Tasse 2017. The "Beckham" law is a Spanish tax law that was approved in 2005 (Real Decree 687/2005). The law owes its nickname to the football player David Beckham, one of the first foreigners to take advantage of the possibilities offered by the aforementioned. The Decree, subsequently repealed with an amendment starting in January 2010, provided for a tax rate of 24 percent (24.75% from January 2012) for foreign workers residing in Spain for a well-defined period of time. It was reintroduced by the Rajoy government, but with an important difference: the decree is now applicable exclusively to those who earn less than 600,000.00 Euros. In 2005, the main beneficiaries were precisely those who declared revenues far exceeding €600,000.00 per year. The Spanish tax reform (Ley 26/2014 of November 27) has profoundly changed the special regime for "neo" residents in Spain (or "Impatriados"), provided for in Art. 93 of Law 35/2006. The decree now expressly excludes professional footballers from its scope. Previously, any foreign worker who had been present

COMPARATIVE EXAMINATION OF THE FIGURE OF THE FOOTBALL   49

reintroduction, with profound changes and restrictions, in 2016. The law earned its nickname after David Beckham became one of the first expats in Spain to take advantage of the opportunity to be subject to a flat rate of tax of 24 percent. The intent of the Spanish legislator was clear: to make Spanish football more attractive and competitive for foreign talents. Thus, the best clubs have been able to maximize their revenues thanks to the massive push of television rights to finance their expenses. The same idea, as already mentioned, was given to the Italian clubs, which, with a strong push to the government, have achieved what they have been fighting for: the growth decree mentioned in the previous paragraph.

However, starting from the 2015/2016 season, in Spain, there has been a reversal of the trend regarding the sale of TV rights, compared to the rest of the Big Five, where the rights deriving from the reproduction of the matches on television are sold collectively, as it happens in many other leagues, and therefore, there will be a tendency to reduce the revenue gap between top clubs and low-middle-range clubs, with the intentional consequence of improving the competitive balance between the Spanish clubs. With the previous system of individual rights sales, Barcelona and Real Madrid have earned more than 140 million euros each year from the proceeds from the TV broadcasts of their official matches, thus having an unrivaled competitive advantage at national level from clubs of lesser status. However, the Spanish government pushed for a new law that gave

---

in the country for more than 183 days in a tax year was considered resident from a tax point of view, which meant being subject to the payment of Spanish taxes on income earned in both Spain and abroad. With the introduction of the Beckham Law, an expatriate worker can apply to be taxed as a non-resident under the Spanish rules relating to income taxes for non-residents: this means that the aforementioned worker will only be taxed on income produced in Spain and not on income generated abroad. If the expatriate can take advantage of the above regime, he will be subject to a fixed tax of 24 percent (Fiscal years 2015 and 2016), rather than subject to the progressive tax rates applicable to Spanish residents. If taxed as a resident, the expatriate would be subject to Spanish income tax which is usually levied at source at a rate ranging from 24 to 45 percent. The exemption applies in the year of arrival of the expatriate and the following five tax years, for a total of six years.

the Spanish league control over the collective sale of broadcasting rights in a move to improve the finances of smaller clubs, collect outstanding taxes, and increase competitiveness. The new legislation brings Spanish football in line with PL and Serie A. General economic conditions in Spain have also impacted the transfer market over the past decade, with some clubs hit hard by the post-2008 financial crisis and where several of these have been forced to seek financial protection from local credit institutions, to avoid bankruptcy. However, this situation was exacerbated by the critical conditions in the banking system on which the clubs relied for financial support. Back in 2003, the Spanish government enacted a new insolvency law, the Ley Concursal,[12] which allowed companies to defer their outstanding payments to keep their business going.

The general economic situation of the country led 27 Spanish clubs to renegotiate their debts between 2003 and 2014. It is no coincidence, in the light of the above, that in December 2013, the EC took a series of disciplinary actions against seven Spanish clubs for possible favorable tax treatments received from the state, aid for the construction of new stadiums and loans and bank guarantees from regional administrations. In these conditions, where financial solidity has sometimes been difficult to ensure, new sources of financing have come to light. In particular, the TPO agreements already supported by investment funds have proliferated enormously in Spain, operating as an entry point into the football transfer markets, for investors using innovative forms of investment such as the DSI fund, a subsidiary of "Doyen Group," which in the first phase of its activity, invested about 100 million euros in the football sector, becoming the most recognized private investment fund in the sector. DSI's investment strategy has increased brand awareness in the average football player, enabling it to position itself as a serious and credible financial player for the football industry, working closely with many teams including: Atletico Madrid, Benfica, Porto, Seville, and Twente FC.

---

[12] Ley Concursal(or Bankruptcy law): "The insolvency law is the name used to designate the set of substantive and procedural rules governing the insolvency procedures of all types of debtors (natural or legal persons)."

The Market of Agents and Intermediaries in France

France, among the five sisters, is certainly the one with the least media impact and competitiveness of its internal championship. This role of *Serie B* was placidly accepted by factual evidence until the end of the 80s, when the French clubs eliminated the old system of making the market protectionist, and therefore, exclusively internal, to open up to the rest of Europe. With the proliferation of more and more international operations, the FFF produced the first national sports agents regulation in 1992.[13] The first national regulatory framework, however, soon proved ineffective because it was able to function exclusively hand in hand with the FIFA license, of international derivation. This necessary regulatory duplicity has led to its rapid application complexity in practice, so much so as to push the French national legislature to issue a second and much more complex regulation for agents in 2000; the Code du Sport. Its articles regulate the sports agency, in particular article R131-18,[14] and incorporate a licensing system organized by the FFF, with further rigorous reviews in 2010. In a survey carried out by the FFF itself, in 2018, only 15 percent of prospective agent candidates were able to obtain the FFF license to act as official agents. as evidence of the extremely technical origin of the profession; rules of international law, civil and community law, follow and intersect very frequently with each other. The eye of the reader must be trained to pass easily to their application in practice. In line with a stringent and careful regulation of the figure, the FFF has finally expressly obliged each individual agent to report the list of all the operations and all his clients to the federation. In 2014, the official census recorded 338 official agents in France. With the approval of the FIFA brokerage system wanted by Blatter, with the domino effect of de facto opening access to

---

[13] For the Regulation: "https://fff.fr/la-fff/agents-sportifsfff/agents-autres"

[14] Code du sport, FFF, 2000, Article R131-18: "La durée des missions de conseillers techniques sportifs ne peut excéder quatre ans. Ces missions sont renouvelables. Le ministre chargé des sports peut mettre fin à ces missions avant le terme fixé, de sa propre initiative ou, le cas échéant, à la demande de l'agent ou du président de la fédération, sous réserve du respect d'un préavis prévu dans la convention-cadre mentionnée à R. 131-23. Toutefois, en cas d'urgence, il peut être mis fin sans préavis à ces missions."

the profession in the 2015 to 2017 two-year period, the FFF has decided to adopt an internal protectionist system, trying not to demean the high quality standard required until shortly before for access to the profession of agent, attributing to the French licenses already issued, valid until the summer of 2020. While foreign agents helping top clubs have previously been an anomaly in this transfer market, the current trend is changing and looks set to continue. According to Bertrand Gardon, president of the UNFP[15] football association, "the fact that the market is completely open favors the arrival of stronger foreign intermediaries, who earn exorbitant commissions." In June 2013, before the Council of State, the two associations of French agents filed an appeal against the cap on commissions of 6 percent imposed by the Executive Committee of the FFF, under pressure from the association of clubs UCPF[16] (France Football, 2013). For the first time, the UASF and SNAS[17] worked together and the fee limit was removed. However, a similar 10 percent limit for gross wages below €1.8 million per year remains today.

The Market for Agents and Intermediaries in Germany

Let's start with an assumption: the Bundesliga is the most followed football league in the world. For years now, German clubs have established a special bond with their supporters, so much so that their supporters are an active part in their way of doing football business. A bit like in England, supporters are very anchored to geographical criteria, often cheering on the club in their city or in the main urban center closest to them. Unlike English football though, where ticket prices are often similar to what you

---

[15] The National Union of Professional Footballers or UNFP is a union formed on November 16, 1961 by two footballers, Eugène N'Jo Léa (then a young law graduate), Just Fontaine, and a lawyer, Maître Jacques Bertrand. It is the main union of French professional footballers. Its current president is Philippe Piat. He shares the presidency with Sylvain Kastendeuch.

[16] The Union of Professional Football Clubs (UCPF) is a union of the presidents of professional football clubs. The UCPF was created on February 28, 1990 as an association law of 1901 under the name of Union of Professional Football Clubs.

[17] SNAS is an acronym that stands for the French "National Union of Sports Agents."

buy to go to the theater, in the Bundesliga Ticket prices are kept low with an effort by clubs to support their local football communities.

One of the secrets of the profitability of the German league is due to strict ownership rules that guarantee a solid local community to be able to assert their ideas in decision making with the management. A sort of popular shareholding. This mentality is typical of German professional football, where the will is to prevent a single person from being able to control the fate of an entire club, of an entire community, therefore, without worrying about historical relationships and ties between clubs, fans, and players themselves. The legal formula chosen is that of registered non-profit associations, and as such, the so-called verein, that is, some clubs, are required by law to hold at least 50 percent plus one of the club's voting rights. Vereins, such as Hamburger Sport-Verein to name one, are run by representatives elected by members, who are usually fans, of the local football community. This results in a special structure that is not authorized to distribute any profits to representatives or members of the club or even less, to sell individual club membership rights. However, there is a strong tendency for club representatives to reinvest all available funds.

A positive aspect, in some ways (as long as the German football economy works) and negative in others, is given by the structure of most German clubs, which therefore heavily discourages external investors and foreign properties that in fact in other leagues, as already mentioned (e.g., Italy), have often saved historic clubs from bankruptcy. These aspects could lead German clubs to adopt more moderate transfer strategies than other leagues, favoring the domestic market with the exception of Bayern Munich, which usually buys foreign players and coaches (FIFA TMS 2014). With an almost always internal management, a very geo-localized market and a club with popular shareholding, it is easy to understand how the world of representation in Germany is absolutely hostile to the entry of foreign intermediaries. But not for a discriminatory reason; simply because there is no reason to consult very often, for example a French agent, for a player who plays in Germany. On the other hand, however, the birth of the new league led to the expansion of the profession of intermediaries within the national market.

The player representation market is highly transparent and agent information is more readily available than in other markets. German agents tend to provide reliable information on their agencies' activity through their social media. For most of the top agencies, you can check the list of their up-to-date clients and how they are organized internally in terms of work teams, functions, and responsibilities of individual employees. In addition, agencies tend to demonstrate which partnerships are established with different service agencies and other football agencies. It is therefore not surprising that the German representation industry has been relatively immune to scandals in the transfer market, suggesting that collaboration between clubs and associations in terms of governance could minimize the impact of opportunistic behaviors on the football brokerage side for agents.

On the other hand, a sector of strong interest for this profession in Germany is the bridge that the nation itself represents between the Eastern European and Western European championships. Consequently, it is quite common to see football agencies developing Central European networks to facilitate player transfers. The agencies "ISMG" and "Soccer Talk," for example, are both linked to the Croatian market through their founder and main agent, Gordon Stipic and Alen Augustincic, respectively. Another example is the "Stars & Friends" founded in early 2005 by the merger of the Austrian "Star Factory" and the German agency "Strunz & Friends." The company operates in Central European markets with offices in Austria, Germany, Slovakia, Norway, and Hungary.

Agents with the Highest Market Power Worldwide. Conclusions

Concluding the analysis now carried out, we can mention some of the most famous agencies worldwide, using once again the numerical data obtained from the research carried out by Rossi, Semens, and Brocard in their work "Sports Agents and labor Markets."

England, as mentioned, is the most economically important nation in terms of commissions for agents, with the first British agency is the "Stellar Group," ranked third in the ranking of the top 50 agencies worldwide, with a potential transfer of income of around €200 million. On the Forbes list, the agency ranks 10th with a portfolio of 143 athletes, worth an estimated €392 million in transfer fees and around €40 million in commissions. The other major British agency, "Base Soccer," is ranked sixth with players worth around €145 million in the market. Their clients include Brazilian internationals Felipe Anderson and Norberto Neto. In fourth position with 198 million euros is the American "WMG." The company is a global agency representing 410 athletes in 20 sports around the world. According to Forbes, the entire company ranks fourth in the top 50 sports agencies with around €2.1 billion in contracts for athletes and around €101 million in commissions. The Italian agencies are the most numerous, with a diversified market. In Spain, the agencies are strongly influenced by Real Madrid and Barcelona, carrying out in the other cases a series of operations in a minor tone, which, however, does not see them as protagonists on the international scene. In Germany, on the other hand, we are witnessing a peculiar phenomenon, in sharp contrast to the rest of Europe where, except for the bridge with Central European countries, the German agent market remains decidedly closed to international trade.

Historical Excursus on the Figure of the Football Agent

The sports agent, and in particular the football agent, in the light of the analysis just concluded has become a very significant figure in the business of contemporary sport. The key role played by the agent is essential to our understanding of labor markets and employment relationships in an increasingly globalized sports industry. Offering analysis from historical, economic, and social perspectives, this final part of the chapter explores key topics such as:

- The history of sports agents
- The emergence of the modern agent in the current football sport model

The development of football as an industrial model led, in the 20th century, to the creation of completely new professional categories and roles. Among these, football agents have undoubtedly emerged as the most powerful entrepreneurial category among the various stakeholders in the sector, operating as the negotiation bridge between players and clubs. In controlling players and in some cases also having control over certain clubs, football agents are certainly responsible for a significant part of the creation of the modern football economic landscape. Although football agents have been socially recognized as representatives since the early 20th century, their role (and regulation) didn't formally crystallize until 1994, when FIFA issued its first rules to govern them. Since then, public authorities and government bodies have tried to identify and control this profession from a legal and economic point of view.

With the formal recognition by FIFA, a classification and a more rigorous definition of the roles, duties, and responsibilities assumed by those who seek to take care of the interests of professional footballers in a 360° management in which to be protected has arrived, they are often also profiles of an athlete's social security, welfare, and entrepreneurial nature. To understand how and why the modern football industry has developed also thanks to the professional figure in question, it is good to first remember what is meant by the term *agent*. In fact, the words *agent* and *intermediary* are often used erroneously interchangeably in the common football language, but in reality, between the two denominations, there have traditionally been subtle differences, already detailed in the previous Chapter 1, under the civil law aspect and regulate. This distinction, however, can again help us explain the development of the football economic sector. Professor Frenkiel,[18] of the CIES institute maintains in its paper (of which a free English translation of the original text in French is shown) that:

> [I]n the business context, both terms are defined as professionals who act with or between two or more commercial parties for legitimate economic activities, offered by a supplier to a consumer. However, while agents are legally authorized to act on behalf of either party by concluding a specific contract, intermediaries mainly carry out only material actions (establishing contracts,

---

[18] International Center for Sports Studies: "has its registered office in Neuchatel, Switzerland, and is an institution that conducts research mainly on the cost of international transfers in the football field. Born from a joint venture between FIFA, the city of Neuchatel and its university."

organizing meetings, etc.) in order to bring the contracting parties together and, as such, they tend to have a less formal relationship with their clients.

In many ways, without knowing the technicalities of the relationships in place, it is impossible to distinguish the work of the two figures and to a certain extent the terms are therefore used interchangeably. Whatever the position prior to FIFA's creation of the intermediary in football, the roles of the new intermediaries and old agents cannot be distinguished from each other in practical terms. This paragraph explores the circumstances through which the football agent industry has developed globally, through a transition of football agents from a practical and improvised activity, devoid of any official status, to a coveted, legally recognized profession, central to the operations of world football markets. This parable can be traced through three periods, which reflect respectively the birth, the exponential growth, and in parallel, the liberalization of the labor markets and the transfer of players.

We can thus highlight a first period that goes from the end of the 19th century to the end of the 1950s, characterized mainly by scouting and brokerage activities on behalf of clubs;

A second moment that instead starts from the early 60s and arrives in the mid-90s, where the representation of footballers as known today under different profiles was born.

Up to a third historical phase, which starts from the mid-90s up to the very recent topicality, which has already been extensively treated in the first chapter of the book, characterized by a real professionalization of football agents, obviously saving the brief as unfortunate parenthesis of the cd Liberalization of football agents, following the declared will of the now former president (following the corruption scandal) of FIFA, Joseph Blatter.

From the end of the 19th century to the end of the 1950s: scouting and brokerage on behalf of clubs

Market intermediaries, or football agents, have existed since the beginning of the game of football, originally playing scouting and recruiting roles for clubs. In a phase immediately following the beginning of this activity, the clubs decided to try to reduce commission costs, therefore salary with much lower salaries, figures capable of performing the same service but as employees of the club. In this way, the scouting networks inside the clubs are expanding, almost eliminating the role of intermediaries from the international football scene. These changes in the market, operated unilaterally by the clubs, have led intermediaries to seek new ways to *recycle* their job position, starting to work as a bridge between players and clubs. The component relating to the *intimate*, individual, informal knowledge that the agent will assert against the clubs that intend to acquire the professional sports performance of an athlete will be increasingly greater. A first formal recognition of the figure, albeit *a contrary* was obtained in 1936, precisely at the 23rd FIFA Congress, which prohibited the use of intermediaries in transfers, believing that they could encourage the development of illegal practices against clubs, for the sole purpose to increase the net salary of their clients. This gloomy vision of intermediaries, resisted until the 1960s, when this figure became in effect an *agent*, as it is known today, radically changing the approach to a profession, which was previously based on the spasmodic search for a compromise that basically satisfied all the parties to the contract, that is, player, club, and obviously intermediary, was now based on the direct and exclusive representation of the athletes, with the well-declared objective for the agent, to try to reach the best economic solution for his client, no longer caring about the interests of the club than with *his* athlete, he was negotiating. Sports agents, mind you, not football, emerged even before the 23rd FIFA Congress, in the most profitable U.S. sports.

At the time of the American Civil War [19] (1861–1865), professional baseball teams, one of the most popular sports in the nation with stars and stripes, were itinerant, and not having a private stadium were promoted by various intermediaries, managers, men of experience, and contacts, who offered wealthy entrepreneurs the idea of starting their own professional baseball team, acquiring the rights of one of the existing touring

---

[19] The American Civil War, known in the United States as the "American Civil War," was fought from April 12, 1861 to April 9, 1865 between the United States of America and the Confederate States of America.

companies.[20] Although their role was specific to each particular case, they typically financed the production of a particular tour or event in order to generate future revenue from tickets and commercial sales. In contrast to the developing football market in Europe, agents in the United States have been recognized as facilitators of these new and popular forms of entertainment and, as such, their role has been widely accepted. The U.S. government, as we will see in Chapter 3 below, has given the sport a certain level of autonomy by choosing not to intervene and has allowed individual promoters and organizers to enjoy considerable independence. This space offered entrepreneurs, agents, the opportunity to profit from initiatives that were very avant-garde for their time. Against the backdrop of increased commercialization in sport, athletes realized they could potentially earn more if they had the help of an experienced negotiator. A man who knew of extra sporting dynamics, who had ties almost everywhere. One more weapon. This is how the sports agent is seen in the United States.

A pioneer, if not the founder of the figure of the sports agent in the sense we give him today, is Charles C. Pyle, commonly known as "Cash & Carry" Pyle, credited as the first sports agent. He, a theater promoter, had managed in 1925 to negotiate a contract worth about $3,000 for each single event for Harold "Red" Grange with the Chicago Bears, along with over $300,000 in film rights and additional bonuses. Pyle represented other major athletes in the 1920s and 1930s[21] and is an icon of the multifaceted profession of the sports agent.

But if we want to give further prestige, perhaps in a decisive way, to the figure of the sports agent, mind you, not yet football, Christy Walsh, a sportswriter, a calm person, thought about it unwittingly. Certainly not a practicing lover of games to raise, Walsh was hired by New York Yankees baseball player "Babe" Ruth as his advisor—yes, but with a predominant focus on the financial side, to help him with contract negotiations, and this marked a shift in the way agents were viewed in the

---

[20] Zeiler. T.W. 2007. "Basepaths to Empire: Race and the Spalding World Baseball Tour." *The Journal of the Gilded Age and Progressive Era* 6, no. 2, pp. 179–207.
[21] Cfr. Masteralexis, L.P., C.A. Barr, and M.A. Hums, III ed. 2009. *Principles and Practice of Sport Management.* Jones and Bartlett Publishers.

landscape. Professional sportsman. Thus, while U.S. sports agents, acting as promoters and intermediaries, were able to openly exploit commercial opportunities in the creation of leagues and other competitions, gaining ground, the same path was not viable in the UK, where football was born and immediately became the most popular sport strictly controlled by the existing state football authorities, of which there are still traces today with the FA (the English Football Association, the oldest world football federation). As in many revolutions brought by the Americans, so also in this case, it took about twenty years compared to the American "cousins," to see the birth of the sports agent, first in England until it took hold throughout the European continent. Their role was initially largely limited to advising clubs on how to find new football talents, an activity that was then split and currently still carried out by the scout. Although the first case of professionalism in football dates back to 1876, with the transfer of the player James Lang to Sheffield Wednesday, the English FA tried to curb the birth of professionalism until 1885, when at the end of a strong debate between all the interpreters of the game of football, reluctantly sanctioned its professionalization. In this way, we quickly passed from a recruitment still based on referral fees, to literally sponsored recruitment on the press media. As we will see in the last chapter in more detail, the link between agents and the *fourth estate* that of the media has always been complementary. These two figures, journalist and agent, seem so to speak, made to work hand in hand. J. Paul Campbell from the city of Liverpool is remembered, as quoted in his 1999 writing by the historian Taylor, for being the first agent to promote some players in clubs through newspaper advertising, starting this unusual and effective sponsorship of his assisted, in March 1891. The type of intermediaries that was created was mostly made up of small entrepreneurs, people who had a second job at the beginning of the profession, who recognized and were able to exploit the lack of corporate organization in the first professional clubs.

In the early 20th century, agents suffered a drastic blow to their profession, which almost cast doubt on their survival: in fact, clubs began to take responsibility for recruiting players for their club, giving rise to the figure of the *football observer (or scout)*, and the activity of the agents decreased dramatically. Furthermore, the FA believed that the agents were against an ethical view of football, turning it into a race for the best bargain and did not approve of their profession, to the point that the activities of individuals attempting to profit as intermediaries for clubs and players so officially prohibited. However, although the clubs were regularly advised not to deal with agents, there was still a strong demand from the companies for their services precisely because these figures were recognized as having an effective ability to evaluate the best *hidden gems* on the national territory. Regardless of their controversial image, the growth, and increasing openness of the international transfer market has given agents the opportunity to start gaining both visibility and prominent positions in the development of football. Since their inception, all the professional leagues have imported foreign players in accordance with their respective domestic transfer market restrictions. In Europe, however, restrictions on the import of foreign players were particularly widespread. In 1933, the German federation imposed a general ban on foreign players and managers, while in Italy, only foreign players with dual citizenship from South America, the so-called *oriundi*, could play. Since 1931, foreign players in England must have lived in the country for at least two years, before the FA recognized them as residents. Their number has therefore remained limited and for those few, there was often a space of mere amateur football, far from the blazon and the salaries of professionalism in which most British footballers resided. French football saw strong growth after World War I, with the spread of amateur leagues. As its popularity grew, the revenue from matches also increased. It has gradually become established practice for clubs to reimburse expenses and award prizes to players based on their sporting achievements. Gradually, football has taken hold in traditionally working-class areas with many players from mining regions and with a strong contingent of Polish and Italian migrants. At the time, players could change clubs at will, thus giving a very strong propulsive boost to the creation of a role similar to that of the agent seen in England in supporting the recruitment of clubs by British agents. The recruitment of players from abroad has also started to spread in stark contrast to the English case.

A phenomenon that has given a decisive boost to the overtaking on the football scene of the figure in question is given by the international football and non-football governments, which begin to allow clubs, as happened in France in the late 1930s, to being able to field up to five foreign players in each match. This and other similar regulations throughout Europe, contribute significantly to the hiring, by the most important clubs, of intermediaries from abroad to find players wishing to emigrate. In turn, the clubs giving away athletes in France have seen a clear utility in the activity of intermediaries in helping them to make the most of by transferring the most talented players to other clubs for adequate payment. This asymmetric information that was created at the beginning between the French clubs (in possession of the professional services of foreign agents, advisor of the real qualities of a player at the time of purchase) and the foreign club of purchase of the player (unaware of the real potential and/or physical condition of the athlete) has also allowed some intermediaries to make money by transferring players from France to foreign clubs, well below the minimum quality level required to play in such a league.[22] At the end of the Second World War, intermediaries were widespread in all major European football markets. However, most of the players were not yet officially followed by an agent in the transfer operations or in the contract renewal phases. Players at that time were seen exclusively as bargaining chips, pawns to be moved at the club's will, without adequate labor legislation to protect their welfare and social security rights. Competition from foreign leagues with a strong desire to contract the highest-profile players has offered tempting alternatives to local football. This tendency to *expatriate* was also aggravated by the presence of a salary cap, present both in France and in England, which remained in force until 1961 and in fact, made it more difficult for the clubs of these countries to excel in race to grab the best talents mainly from South America. Consequently, in the 1950s and 1960s, the most promising or established players often moved to Italy, where similar regulatory constraints were not present, and did so through agents who became increasingly closely involved in the negotiations between clubs and players, to mostly British. These include John Charles's move from Leeds United to Juventus in 1957, due to the involvement of Teddy Sommerfield, whose other clients

---

[22] Cfr. Whal, D.N., and M.P. Lanfranchi. 1995. *Les footballeurs professionnels:Des années trente à nos jours*. Ed. La vie quotidienne actuelles.

included television celebrities such as Eamonn Andrews, and show business personalities. It was the first time a British player had hired an agent
to facilitate his move overseas. At that time, the most famous broker was
Gigi Peronace, referred to as the *real agent* or *Italian man* in England,
he worked part-time as a scout and broker in the Anglo-Italian transfer
market for several clubs, such as Chelsea, Manchester United, Lazio,
Turin, Juventus, and Milan. The clubs thus began to see their bargaining
power eroded, given the increasingly frequent push of agents in favor
of their clients, but above all, the figure of the agent began to become
in great demand (and still is today) in the categories of players, less
well-off, those who certainly cannot afford a serious or trivial injury, to
remain a year without a team.

This information in itself would not be so relevant for historical
purposes were it not that this category of players represents about 90
percent of the entire global athlete landscape. From the early 1940s,
intermediaries began organizing friendly matches between clubs or tour-
naments that served as a showcase for their clients. All the clubs that
have identified a potential transfer target in one of these matches therefore negotiate directly with the club that holds the player's sports rights,
the possible amount of the deal. Since player representation was still
prohibited, intermediaries were paid fees in connection with the organization of the match and for this reason, in 1969, UEFA decided to create
a license for match agents, that is, organization of matches recognized as
official, and monitoring their activity by giving life to the figure of the
UEFA match agent. In Spain, the first generation of football intermediaries started operating in the 1940s and 1950s. Again, asymmetrical
information, this time with South American clubs, implied that some
intermediaries were exploiting the transfer market with scandals like
"el timo de los orioundos," in which South American players had to
forge their passports to obtain Spanish citizenship. and, subsequently,
moving to Spanish clubs.

In Italy, the so-called Calciomercato, the official transfer market for
footballers, was founded by the Prince of Trabia, Raimondo Lanza who,
at that time, in the 1950s, was president of Palermo Calcio. It has turned
into an annual gathering where club owners, club directors, and brokers

meet to hold player buying and selling meetings at the Hotel Gallia in Milan.[23]

From the early 1960s to the mid-1990s: the representation of footballers

By 1960, it had become apparent in England that labor market restrictions were not conducive to retaining the best players. The salary cap, an idea that sounds dated in today's football world, shouldn't come as a surprise when you think about the current NBA salary cap. In any case, the players union, the PFA was using its political influence to try to arrive at a rule that at least put England back in a position to counter Italy's excessive power in the field of acquisitions of the best players on the world scene. The British FA's 1961 decision to abolish the maximum wage balanced the bargaining power between players and clubs to the point where most athletes began negotiating their contracts with the assistance of personal agents. In making player transfers more flexible, leagues and football federations have legitimized the use of intermediaries. However, there were still important restrictions on the free movement of players from one club to another as clubs, at the time, could unilaterally extend player contracts as long as they are offered economic terms equal to their previous contract; in essence, it meant tying a player to the club for as long as the player was willing to pay for his services, regardless of whether the player wished to stay in that club. In France, a similar reform process was underway, led by Just Fontaine who, following the examples of his English colleagues, founded the French footballers' union, the UNFP, in 1961 and immediately began negotiations with representatives of the clubs that led to the signing of the first collective agreement, which as a corollary introduced the reform of the pension system in November 1964. In 1969, the UNFP had given rise to a real revolution; challenging the consolidated legal framework of the labor market of the time, he was able to negotiate for the first time the possibility for players and clubs to enter into *fixed*

---

[23] Cfr. "have to dance" by Ottavia Casagrande, Raimonda Lanza di Trabia, Ed. La Feltrinelli 2017: "He has a unique way of conducting his negotiations: Immersed in the bathtub of a suite of the Hotel Gallia in Milan, with a jug of coffee on one side and an immense crème caramel on the other, he received the presidents of the other teams, negotiated, gave in, exchanged. He thus 'invented' the transfer market."

term contracts. Under this system, a player can only be registered with a club for a limited period of time, which may be the subject of future negotiation and which cannot be less than three years for an amateur player who signs his first professional contract and not even a year in any other case, which meant that at the end of his contract, a player could negotiate with any club without the opposition of his former home club.

With the growth of the European system both politically and as a commercial market, it was necessary to create a homogeneous and standard transfer system, which did not prejudice rights obtained in this or that nation. This need gave rise to a confederate system, that of UEFA, which was able to allow the free movement of players nationally and internationally.

This UEFA system has set a maximum transfer fee limit. On February 23, 1978, in Brussels, the football federations of various European countries and the Executive Committee of the EEC met to establish the principle of free movement of players within the borders of the EEC member states. At the same time, with the opening of markets to all of Europe, media interest in sport as part of regular television programming has expanded very rapidly, bringing huge amounts of revenue to leagues. As the activities of sports agents have begun to become more widely recognized, their numbers have increased exponentially and individuals from diverse backgrounds and professions have entered the industry. Similarly, the increase in revenue available to players has resulted in a change in the type of advice required, as legal and financial support has become necessary. These new services, which tended to be available only through personal consultants, became a necessity, so as to increasingly favor the arrival of professionals from different economic sectors not previously involved in the world of sport.

CHAPTER 3

The Peculiar Regulation of the Football Agents in the USA

Historical Notes on the Birth of the Figure in the United States and its Legal Framework

The North American sources of sports law are generally in agreement in attributing, as already mentioned in the previous chapters, to Charles Pyle the title of first sports attorney in the history of the sport. In 1926, in fact, Pyle negotiated a contract worth a hundred thousand dollars for Harold Grange, a football player at the University of Illinois.

However, until the first half of the seventies, a certain hostility toward this figure can be recorded on the part of the interlocutors' par excellence of the agents, the sports directors, who almost refused to give the dignity of professionals to this figure who came of against bound to the concept of mere *practitioner*, a figure who without some skills, tried to grab a part of the athlete's salary against the club, which, on the other hand, saw the economic outlays to be incurred in every negotiation rise. It seems right that the basis of the change that led to a rapid rise in the role of the agent, there were strictly sporting reasons, such as the progressive acquisition of power in bargaining by athletes, as well as motivations related to more general reasons, such as the ever-increasing acquisition of visibility by some sports and the consequent need to manage this popularity by the athletes themselves. In fact, athletes with the advent of television and radio began to lend their voice or, more generally, their image for commercials, TV programs, sales of food products and clothes signed by big brands. All this popularity could no longer be handled by the sportsman alone, and if it was done, professional performance on the pitch could often suffer.

Indeed, in the face of a reality in which in the United States a new professional figure was progressively imposing itself, and in consideration of the numerous problems that it was suddenly posing to the interpreter, the same federal and state institutions, and the major student sports organizations, such as the NCAA,[1] noted the need to intervene to guarantee and promote a substantial reorganization of this figure.

The opportunity resulted in the drafting and subsequent approval of the Uniform Athlete Agents Act (UAAA), the first regulatory intervention on the subject, aimed at uniform regulation of the figure of the sports agent. Although, in fact, already in the eighties, the National Football League Players Association had suggested the need, together with other trade associations, to adopt a common legislative text, and despite 29 states having accepted this invitation by promulgating a sort of *code of conduct* for agents, however, these interventions, while appreciable, they were not very incisive in terms of general regulation, given the absence of legislative coordination and legitimation on the part of the federal government essential to regulatory enforcement.

In this regard, the role of primary importance played by the university sports organizations in persuading institutions to definitively address the issue should be noted, as the intervention of the NCAA demonstrates, where it obtained the formal intervention of the National Conference of Commissioners on Uniform State Laws.[2]

---

[1] NCAA, *National Collegiate Athletic Association*, cfr. sito ufficiale, www.ncaa.org

[2] The National Conference of Commissioners on Uniform State Laws (NCCUSL) is a commission established in 1892, on a voluntary basis, for the states that decide to join it. It has the purpose of promoting and coordinating the uniform drafting of legislative texts among the states of the federation. It is made up of about 340 members, representing each state that has joined, including the District of Columbia, Puerto Rico and the North American territories of the Virgin Islands. Generally these are government officials, lawyers, judges, and university professors of law. The commission has drafted more than 250 pieces of legislation, including the fundamental Uniform Commercial Code and the Uniform Probate Code. Also, the American Bar Association. and the American Law Institute, in addition to contributing financially, provide, if requested, their

Any matter taken into consideration by this commission, created with the aim of encouraging intra-state cooperation in the legislative field, must first be examined by a study group (Committee on Scope and Program-CSP), whose task consists in an initial evaluation of the opportunity for a subject to become an object of future interest. In the present case, this commission took office in June 1996 offering a favorable opinion to start drafting a single legislative text.

A first part of the drafting, ready in 1999, in fact, was dedicated to the access procedure and the requisites necessary for the exercise of the profession, while a second part referred to the functional profile of the sport agent, thus taking into consideration the relationship with the athlete-student, the conduct to be observed, and any terms of prosecution of illegal actions.

The Model of the U.S. Sports Agent as an Example for European Football

The second and definitive draft of the Uniform Athlete Agents Act, presented in July 2000 in Florida, does not differ from the previous version except for slight changes in the language used. In regards to the terms of access, the UAAA provides in detail the obligation on the part of the sports attorney to register his name in a sort of professional list in every single state in which he intends to practice the profession, as well as to draw up a specific declaration certifying qualifications and related titles.

It seems useful to highlight how in the text there is no indication of the so-called *minimum standards*, that is to say the requirements that the agent must possess in order to obtain registration.[3]

Finally, the definitive step in the direction of what was hoped for and largely envisaged by the Uniform Athlete Agents Act was taken in 2004

---

own advice through their own experts. See Nat "l conference of comm" rs on unif. state laws, Reference Book, n.8, 2000.

[3] In this regard, see R.N. Davis, cit., "The Committee was not interested in attempting to develop minimum educational or certification requirements for athlete agents because that was viewed as more appropriate for the players associations."

with the approval by Congress of the Sports Agent Responsibility and Trust Act (SPARTA).[4] This legislation, taking up the general structure and the provisions of the Uniform Athlete Agents Act, strengthened by the federal legitimacy conferred by Congress, presents an element of novelty represented by the attribution to the Federal Trade Commission of the power to intervene in the hypothesis of *deceptive acts or practice*[5] by the agent.

In view of its general scope, as a federal legislation, the Sports Agent Responsibility and Trust Act also represents an essential regulatory aid in states where the Uniform Athlete Agents Act has not been transposed.[6]

In fact, this idea is confirmed by the different legal nature (and scope) of the two different regulations. While the UAAA, consisting of a non-federal rule, in which therefore each federal state, in total discretion can decide to choose whether or not to adopt a legislative text, the SPARTA, as mentioned above, strengthened by the qualification of federal law and, therefore, characterized by binding effectiveness for all states of the federation, it represents a clear and manifest awareness on the part of the national legislator in the field of sports agents.

In fact, it starts from a more general consideration regarding the attitude that government institutions, on the one hand, and sports organizations, on the other, have taken on the sporting phenomenon. Although sport, as a matter of local, state, and federal interest, plays a leading role, also endorsed by the copious jurisprudence on the subject and by the numerous contributions coming from the doctrine, however, it has never reached an institutional root like an autonomous legal entity. A further consideration must be made, then, with regard to the perception of the

---

[4] *Sports Agent Responsibility and Trust Act (SPARTA)*, 15 USC §7801.

[5] https://nclc.org/issues/unfair-a-deceptive-acts-a-practices.html

[6] It is recalled, in fact, that the UAAA, to date, has been approved by 38 states of the federation. See Sports Agent Responsibility and Trust Act: Hearing on H.R. 361 before the Subcomm. on Commercial and Admin. Law of the H. Comm. On the Judiciary, 108th Cong. 4 (May 15, 2003); Rogers, R.M. 2002. *The Uniform Athlete Agent Act Fails to Fully Protect the College Athlete Who Exhausts His Eligibility Before Turning Professional in Villanova Sports & Ent. L.J.*, n. 2, p. 63.

sporting phenomenon by the sporting organizations themselves. Indeed, except in isolated cases, there is no attempt to consider the *specificity* of sport as a cause of justification for the non-application of state or federal legal regulations in order to create real areas of immunity.

In this *order of ideas*, therefore, a substantial balance between the sporting perspective and the state (or federal) legal system is highlighted; a balance that, in the present case, found a complete synthesis, as seen above, with the drafting of the Uniform Athlete Agents Act and subsequently of the Sports Agent Responsibility and Trust Act respectively.

It is also interesting to observe, with regard to the question relating to the application of antitrust legislation in the event that the functions of sports attorney are exercised by a person qualified to practice forensics, which, to date, in the United States poses no limitations in this sense, so that the market offers the possibility, for an athlete, to use a non-attorney agent as much as an attorney agent.[7]

On this point, the doctrine focused on the question concerning the consequences, on the level of professional responsibility and, more generally, on the antitrust level, deriving from unfair conduct and in general outside the "professional ethics, carried out by the sports agent or by the lawyer working as an agent." While, in fact, in the latter case, the rules to refer to on the subject are those established by the state and federal lawyer associations (American Bar Association)[8] and, among the possible

---

[7] In this regard, see, among others, G.P. Kohn, "Sports Agents Representing Professional Athletes: Being Certified Means Never Having to Say You're Qualified," in Ent. & Sports Law, 1988, n.6, p.1-15; SM Nahrwold, "Are Professional Athletes Better Served By a Laywer- Representative Than an Agent? Ask Grant Hill," in Seton Hall J. Sport L., 1999, n. 9, p. 431 ff.

[8] All those who have obtained the qualification to practice forensics are subject to the code of ethics, Model Rules of Professional Conduct, as issued by the American Bar Association and implemented by states and courts. This model therefore also applies to lawyers who work as sports attorneys. With regard to the issue in question, there were those who, in legal literature, suggested modifying the rules of conduct for those who act as prosecutors in a more bland sense. In this regard, mention is made of the so-called Two-Hat Theory, a theory that supports the non-applicability of the rules of professional conduct when the lawyer acts as a

sanctions, there is also the revocation of the license to exercise the profession, the same cannot be said for the first case. According to some of the doctrine, this would create a real *competitive imbalance* in the market, with the consequence of lowering the ethical level of sports representation and damaging effects. According to the same doctrine, it does not take much to realize that ethically incorrect sports agents compete unfairly with respect to attorneys who, on the contrary, behave, at least theoretically, according to the rules of the Bar.

The fact that we have focused on the existence of an effective gap of a competitive nature between the agent and the lawyer, who acts as an agent, is relevant since it denotes the perspective through which one looks at the figure of the sports agent, namely that competitive aspect. Moreover, it should be noted that, despite the importance of this aspect, the legislative text of the Sport Responsibility and Trust Act does not address this problem in any way, even if, as part of the doctrine observed, the provisions of this legislation could be traced to those of the American Bar Association's Model Rule of Professional Conduct. According to this opinion, in fact, the structure of SPARTA has numerous similarities with that of the forensic code of conduct to the point that, it has been said, one of the unintended effects of its enforcement would consist in a *raising* of the level of professional ethics, which *would force* sports agents who are not lawyers to adapt to this level, thus eliminating the competitive gap mentioned.

---

sports attorney. In this sense, see DS Caudill, cit., note 42. Le Model Rules, however, establish that the lawyer engaged in fields other than that of forensic practice is in any case bound to respect the rules of conduct. Also, the jurisprudence confirms this orientation in *In re Dwight,* 573 P.2d 481, 484 (Arizona, 1978) case in which the court ruled that a lawyer, albeit in the capacity of financial advisor, remains subject to the principles of professional ethics established by the ABA. In the same sense, *In re Horak,* 647 NYS2d, where to a lawyer who cited his role as sports attorney as a justification for having behaved badly, the court replied that his qualification was "attorney" and, as such , subject to the related ethical rules to be according to this way.

Beyond these considerations, what I want to highlight once again concerns the profile linked to the uniqueness and uniformity of the Sport Responsibility and Trust Act. It is precisely this character that has proved to be the fundamental starting point for addressing the problem of the football agent, as a professional, in a constructive way.

The North American experience, indeed, although it has not yet provided a solution on the matter, enjoys an advantage, at least on a theoretical level, namely the adoption of a unitary regulation on the subject, strongly desired by sports organizations, but at the same time shared by the central government to the point of giving it the character of federal law.

It is, therefore, to be considered that precisely this advantage represents the fundamental and indispensable prerequisite for a reform of the figure of the sports agent, which also takes into account the competitive perspective, and in so doing, does not remain anchored to an exclusive sports perspective.

It seems to allow us to affirm that the North American perspective is based on a principle: the observation plane from which to observe and analyze different legal phenomena is, and must remain, the competitive one, since the only one, to date, able to ensure equality of conditions to the actors and consequently transparency on the market.

The solution that the author of the text embraces and also suggests at the European level, is to adopt a unitary and homogeneous regulation also in the European context, where football in many nations represents the third sector of the country's economy, thus avoiding the use of mutually inconsistent regulations, which lead only to regulatory chaos and countless appeals by associations, federations, agents, and clubs. In a globalized world market, applying as many regulations as there are individual sports federations belonging to the UEFA confederation seems almost anachronistic and not useful to give vent to the feared need for transparency and fairness, inspiring principles of the reform wanted by FIFA in 2015. In addition to making up for the lack of a unitary regulation shared by the various sports disciplines, a choice in this sense brings the regulation of the sports attorney back to the source that is proper to him, consisting of the state legislator instead of the federal one, given that the sports attorney himself is not considered a subject of the sporting system.

The shift of the regulatory plan from the sports system to the state one implies the affirmation of the application to the figure of the sports attorney of the rules that make up the antitrust legislation. Moreover, the prevalence granted to the heteronomous state source, instead of the federal one, must not lead to the belief that it was intended to deny, or downsize, the character of autonomy that is peacefully recognized in the *sports system*; it was rather wanted to heal the anomaly in progress, consisting in the exclusive regulation by the federal sources of a professional figure who, from the same sources, is considered extraneous to the sports system.

Furthermore, what is proposed should not be interpreted in the sense that the state-based regulation of the figure of the sports agent leads to restricting the scope of exercise of the functions of agent, since this regulation, as already mentioned, must be correlated with the need to apply the rules to safeguard the freedom of work performance also in the professional sector, in which the figure of the sports agent must be included.

The solution proposed by the author of this text would bring a double advantage: from the internal point of view of the sports system, it would put an end to a situation of uncertainty and inhomogeneity, leading to a unitary regulation of the figure of the sports agent regardless of the specific area in which he exercises his activity; from a more general point of view, with regard to the state system as a whole, then, on the assumption that the sports agent or attorney is recognized as a freelancer, it appears in line with the choices adopted in the community and international sphere, that is, the application of the competition rules in the sphere of the professions and, for what concerns us more specifically, of those of a sporting nature.

In this perspective, the system in which the activity corresponding to the competence of the sports attorney takes place must expand, to include all those who, regardless of being registered in a register certifying this competence, are nevertheless in possession of it, guaranteeing thus the same freedom of expression and dynamism of development which, as seen above, represent the peculiar characteristics of the North American system.

The Current Regulation of Agents (intermediaries) in the United States following the FIFA Regulation on Working With Intermediaries of 2015 and the So-Called "Memorandum"

Following the introduction of changes to FIFA's Rules and Regulations in 2015, the United States Soccer Federation (USSF) issued new rules relating to the registration of Soccer Agents (now known as Soccer Intermediaries) wishing to work in the United States. A person wishing to work as an Intermediary in the United States for players or clubs in the MLS must submit an application to the USSF that he be registered as an intermediary. The MLS soccer agent certification process in the United States allows an applicant to either apply to be registered prior to representing a player or club, or while an agent is representing a player or club during the negotiation process with a view to concluding an employment contract or transfer agreement.

The Intermediary Declaration

In order to comply with FIFA Rules & Regulations, the USSF requests that a player and/or club wishing to engage the services of an Intermediary must submit the relevant Intermediary Declaration signed by the Intermediary concerned to the USSF with a copy of the contract entered into by the parties.

The Intermediary Declaration provides as follows:

- To comply with all laws rules and regulations (Clause 1)
- Is of impeccable reputation (i.e., no criminal sentence has ever been imposed upon me for a financial or violent crime) (Clause 3)
- No conflict of interest (Clauses 2 and 4)
- Won't accept a payment owed by one club to another in connection with a transfer (i.e. transfer compensation) (Clause 5)
- Won't accept payment from any party if the player concerned is a minor (Clause 6)

- Won't take part in or be associated with, betting, gambling, lotteries and similar events (Clause 7)
- To the association obtaining full details of any payment of whatsoever nature made to me by a club or a player for my services as an intermediary (Clause 8)
- When the Intermediary is registering for the first time, he must complete the required Declaration and also submit:
- An Intermediary Registration Form and a registration fee of $400.00 via cashier's check or money order to the U.S. Soccer at the following address:

United States Soccer Federation, Inc.
1801 S. Prairie Avenue
Chicago, IL 60616
Attention: Gregory Fike Staff Attorney, U.S. Soccer

Additional Requirements for Intermediaries

Once this application has been submitted, the USSF shall conduct a background check on the applicant to determine if he or she has been convicted of a financial or violent crime. Any Intermediary that is currently registered as a soccer players' agent or who have applied to be a players' agent within the last five years is permitted to submit an application to pre-register by submitting the Intermediary Registration Form and a $50 registration fee via cashier's check or money order to the address above. The fee for renewing Intermediary Registration in the United States is $50 each year.

It is noteworthy that the USSF states that any persons that have been convicted of financial or violent crimes shall not be permitted to register as Intermediaries. The USSF also says that an Intermediary shall not be registered until the Intermediary submits a representation contract between themselves and a player and/or club the agent intends to represent and the other documentation required, and the Intermediary wishing to be registered is involved in the preliminary negotiations of a contract between a player and club.

Learning about the Rules, Regulations, and Laws

It is also advisable that a person who wants to become a football agent learns the basics about the relevant domestic laws, particularly contract law, in the country where he wishes to operate as an agent.

MEMORANDUM TO

Persons Acting as Intermediaries for Players or Clubs

FROM: Gregory Fike Staff Attorney, U.S. Soccer

DATE: March 2015

RE: FIFA Regulations on Working with Intermediaries

This memorandum outlines the procedures for registering as an intermediary with USSF pursuant to FIFA Regulations on Working with Intermediaries ("FIFA Regulations"). All intermediaries, players and clubs must comply with the FIFA Regulations. Under FIFA Regulations, players and clubs are entitled to use the services of an intermediary when completing an employment contract between a player and club or a transfer agreement between two clubs. Intermediaries are any natural or legal persons who, for a fee or free of charge, represent players and/or clubs in negotiations toward concluding an employment contract or transfer agreement. An intermediary to the execution of a player contract or transfer agreement must now register with the USSF, pursuant to the FIFA Regulations. Necessary Submissions when Using Intermediaries: Any player or club engaging the services of an intermediary during the execution of an employment contract or transfer agreement must submit a declaration signed by the intermediary (Appendix A or Appendix B) to USSF upon execution of the employment contract or transfer agreement. Registration of Intermediaries: Aside from the required declaration, intermediaries who have not previously registered with USSF and wish to pre-register as intermediaries must submit (1) an Intermediary Registration Form (Appendix C) (2) and a registration fee of $400.00 via cashier's check or money order to U.S. Soccer at the following address: United States Soccer Federation, Inc. 1801 S. Prairie Avenue Chicago, IL 60616 Attention: Gregory Fike Staff Attorney, U.S. Soccer Intermediaries who have not previously registered with USSF will be subject to a background check to determine if they have ever been convicted of a financial or violent crime. Intermediaries currently registered as players' agents or who have applied to be a players' agent within the last five years may pre-register by submitting the Intermediary Registration Form and a $50 registration fee via cashier's check or money order to the address above. Once registered, intermediaries will need to pay a $50 registration fee each year to maintain their registration. Any persons that have been convicted of financial or violent crimes shall not be permitted to register as intermediaries. If a registered intermediary is convicted of a violent or financial crime, the intermediary must notify USSF of this immediately. Please note that intermediaries shall not actually be registered until the intermediary submits a representation contract between themselves and a player and/or club along with the other required documentation and the intermediary is involved in an executed employment contract or a transfer agreement. Relevant Dates: Intermediaries may pre-register starting April 1, 2015. Pre-registration for the next year will start January 1 of each calendar year in the future. Intermediaries that do not preregister must register upon execution of an employment contract or transfer agreement in which they represent a player or club. Payments and Sanctions: Please see Article 7 of FIFA's Regulations for a guide on proper payment procedures when using intermediaries to execute an employment contract and/or transfer agreement. Sanctions may be imposed on any party under USSF jurisdiction that does not follow the provisions of these registration requirements or the FIFA Regulations. Should you have any additional questions or comments, please do not hesitate to call Greg Fike at (312) 528-1278.

See below for

1. Appendix A: Intermediary Declaration for Natural Persons
2. Appendix B: Intermediary Declaration for Legal Persons
3. Appendix C: Intermediary Registration Form

Appendix A: Intermediary Declaration for Natural Persons First name(s): Last Name(s): Date of birth: Nationality/nationalities: Full permanent address (incl. phone/fax and e-mail)

I, _____

_____ (First name(s), last names(s) of intermediary)

Hereby declare the following:

1. I pledge to respect and comply with any mandatory provisions of applicable national and international laws, including in particular those relating to job placement when carrying out my activities as an intermediary. In addition, I agree to be bound by the statutes and regulations of associations and confederations, as well as by the Statutes and regulations of FIFA in the context of carrying out my activities as an intermediary.

2. I declare that I am currently not holding a position of official, as defined in point 11 of the Definitions section of the FIFA Statutes, nor will I hold such a position in the foreseeable future.

3. I declare that I have an impeccable reputation and in particular confirm that no criminal sentence has ever been imposed upon me for a financial or violent crime.

4. I declare that I have no contractual relationship with leagues, associations, confederations or FIFA that could lead to a potential conflict of interest. In case of uncertainty, any relevant contract shall be disclosed. I also acknowledge that I am precluded from implying, directly or indirectly, that such a contractual relationship with leagues, associations, confederations or FIFA exists in connection with my activities as an intermediary.

5. I declare, pursuant to article 7 paragraph 4 of the FIFA Regulations on Working with Intermediaries, that I shall not accept any payment to be made by one club to another club in connection with a transfer, such as transfer compensation, training compensation or solidarity contributions.

6. I declare, pursuant to article 7 paragraph 8 of the FIFA Regulations on Working with Intermediaries, that I shall not accept any payment from any party if the player concerned is a minor, as defined in point 11 of the Definitions section of the Regulations on the Status and Transfer of Players.

7. I declare that I shall not take part in, either directly or indirectly, or otherwise be associated with, betting, gambling, lotteries and similar events or transactions connected with football matches. I acknowledge that I am forbidden from having stakes, either actively or passively, in companies, concerns, organisations, and so on. that promote, broker, arrange or conduct such events or transactions.

8. I consent, pursuant to article 6 paragraph 1 of the FIFA Regulations on Working with Intermediaries, to the association obtaining full details of any payment of whatsoever nature made to me by a club or a player for my services as an intermediary.

9. I consent, pursuant to article 6 paragraph 1 of the FIFA Regulations on Working with Intermediaries, to the leagues, associations, confederations or FIFA obtaining, if necessary, for the purpose of their investigations, all contracts, agreements and records in connection with my activities as an intermediary. Equally, I consent to the aforementioned bodies also obtaining any other relevant documentation from any other party advising, facilitating or taking any active part in the negotiations for which I am responsible.

10. I consent, pursuant to article 6 paragraph 3 of the FIFA Regulations on Working with Intermediaries, to the association concerned holding and processing any data for the purpose of their publication.

11. I consent, pursuant to article 9 paragraph 2 of the FIFA Regulations on Working with Intermediaries, to the association concerned publishing details of any disciplinary sanctions taken against me and informing FIFA accordingly.

12. I am fully aware and agree that this declaration shall be made available to the members of the competent bodies of the association concerned.

13. Remarks and observations which may be of potential relevance:

_____

_____ I make this declaration in good faith, the truth of which is based on the information and materials currently available to me, and agree that the association concerned shall be entitled to undertake such checks as may be necessary to verify the information contained in this declaration. I also acknowledge that, having submitted this declaration, in the event that any of the abovementioned information changes, I must notify the association concerned   immediately. _____

_____ (Place and date) (Signature)

Appendix B: Intermediary Declaration for Legal Persons

Name of company (legal person/entity): Address of company (incl. phone/fax, e-mail and website): Hereinafter referred to as "the company"

First name(s) and last name(s) of the individual duly authorized to represent the aforementioned company (legal person/entity): (NB: Each individual acting on behalf of the company has to fill in a separate Intermediary Declaration)

I, _____

_____ (First name(s), last name(s) of the individual representing the legal person/ entity) duly authorized to represent the company **Hereby declare the following:**

1. I declare that both the company I represent and that I myself shall respect any mandatory provisions of applicable national and international laws, including in particular those relating to job placement when carrying out activities as an intermediary. In addition, I declare that both the company I represent and that I myself agree to be bound by the statutes and regulations of associations and confederations, as well as by the Statutes and regulations of FIFA in the context of carrying out activities as an intermediary.

2. I declare that I am currently not holding a position of official, as defined in point 11 of the Definitions section of the FIFA Statutes, nor will I hold such a position in the foreseeable future.

3. I declare that I have an impeccable reputation and in particular confirm that no criminal sentence has ever been imposed upon me for a financial or violent crime.

4. I declare that neither the company I represent nor I myself have any contractual relationship with leagues, associations, confederations or FIFA that could lead to a potential conflict of interest. In case of uncertainty, any relevant contract shall be disclosed. I also acknowledge that the relevant company is precluded from implying, directly or indirectly, that such a contractual relationship with leagues, associations, confederations or FIFA exists in connection with its activities as intermediary.

5. I declare, pursuant to article 7 paragraph 4 of the FIFA Regulations on Working with Intermediaries, that neither the company I represent nor I myself shall accept any payment to be made by one club to another club in connection with a transfer, such as transfer compensation, training compensation or solidarity contributions.

6. I declare, pursuant to article 7 paragraph 8 of the FIFA Regulations on Working with Intermediaries, that neither the company I represent nor I myself shall accept any payment from any party if the player concerned is a minor, as defined in point 11 of the Definitions section of the Regulations on the Status and Transfer of Players.

7. I declare that neither the company I represent nor I myself shall take part in, either directly or indirectly, or otherwise be associated with, betting, gambling, lotteries and similar events or transactions connected with football matches. I acknowledge that both the company I represent and I myself are forbidden from having stakes, either actively or passively, in companies, concerns, organisations, and so on. that promote, broker, arrange or conduct such events or transactions.

8. On behalf of the company I represent, I consent, pursuant to article 6 paragraph 1 of the FIFA Regulations on Working with Intermediaries, to the associations obtaining full details of any payment of whatsoever nature made to the company by a club or a player for its services as an intermediary.

9. On behalf of the company I represent, I consent, pursuant to article 6 paragraph 1 of the FIFA Regulations on Working with Intermediaries, to the leagues, associations, confederations or FIFA obtaining, if necessary, for the purpose of their investigations, all contracts, agreements and records in connection with the activities as an intermediary of the company. Equally, I consent to the aforementioned bodies also obtaining any other relevant documentation from any other party advising, facilitating or taking any active part in the negotiations for which the company I represent is responsible.

10. On behalf of the company I represent, I consent, pursuant to article 6 paragraph 3 of the FIFA Regulations on Working with Interme-

diaries, to the association concerned holding and processing any data for the purpose of their publication.

11. On behalf of the company I represent, I consent, pursuant to article 9 paragraph 2 of the FIFA Regulations on Working with Intermediaries, to the association concerned publishing and informing FIFA of any disciplinary sanctions taken against the company I represent.

12. I am fully aware and agree that this declaration shall be made available to the members of the competent bodies of the association concerned.

13. Remarks and observations which may be of potential relevance:

_____

_____ I make this declaration in good faith, the truth of which is based on the information and materials currently available to me, and agree that the association concerned shall be entitled to undertake such checks as may be necessary to verify the information contained in this declaration. I also acknowledge that, having submitted this declaration, in the event that any of the abovementioned information changes, I must notify the association concerned immediately.

_____ (Place and date) _____

(Signature)

Appendix C: United States Soccer Federation Intermediary Registration Form

Instructions: Please provide the information requested below in the spaces provided. Entries should be typed or neatly printed. If more space is needed, please attach extra pages with the information clearly labeled. Upon completion of the application, sign the last page, as well as the attached "Information Release" form.

The completed application should be submitted, along with a $400.00 application fee (in the form of a certified check or money order) to: United States Soccer Federation, Inc. 1801 S. Prairie Avenue Chicago, IL 60616 Attention: Gregory Fike Staff Attorney, US Soccer I. Contact Information (Please provide in this space the information you would like U.S. Soccer to use in contacting you)

Name: _____

_____ Address: _____

_____ City: _____ State: _____

Zip Code: _____ Telephone: _____

Fax: _____ Email: _____

_____ II. Personal Data (Please provide your home address below. If this is the same as your contact information, please indicate "Same as above") Address: _____

_____ City:

_____ State: _____ Zip Code: _____ Tele-

phone: _____ Fax: _____

Date of Birth:_____ Driver's License #:

_____ State: _____ Have you

ever been known by any other name? Yes _____ No _____ If so, list all other names, along with time periods in which you were known by that name: _____

_____ List all residential addresses for the past ten years (in reverse order, most recent first): Address: _____

City: _____ State: _____ Zip: _____ Address:

_____ City: _____ State: _____ Zip:

_____ Address: _____ City: _____

State: _____ Zip: _____ Address: _____ City:

_____ State: _____ Zip: _____ III. Business Information (Only required if applying as a Legal Person rather than a Natural Person) Firm Name: _____

_____ Address: _____ City: _____ State: _____ Zip: _____ Nature of Business: _____

__ Title of Applicant: _____ Date joined/hired: _____ Telephone: _____

Fax: _____ IV. Criminal In the last ten years, have you been convicted of a felony? Yes _____ No _____ If "Yes," please provide the following information about any such convictions: Court: _____ Year: _____ Case #: _____ Charge:_____ Court: _____ Year: _____ Case #: _____ Charge:_____ In the last ten years, have you been convicted of a misdemeanor? Yes _____ No _____ If "Yes," please provide the following information about any such convictions: Court: _____ Year: _____ Case #: _____ Charge:_____ Court: _____ Year: _____ Case #: _____ Charge:_____ V. Current Positions Please answer the following questions: Do you occupy a position with FIFA? Yes _____ No _____ Do you occupy a position with a confederation of FIFA? Yes _____ No _____ Do you occupy a position with any national association? Yes _____ No _____ Do you occupy a position with a league? Yes _____ No _____ Do you occupy a position with an Organization Member of U.S. Soccer? Yes _____ No _____ Do you occupy a position with any club that fields soccer teams? Yes _____ No _____ Do you occupy any position with any organization that is linked with a national association of FIFA ? Yes _____ No _____ Do you occupy a position with U.S. Soccer? Yes _____ No _____

VI. Affirmation I hereby state that the information I have provided in this registration is true, correct, and complete to the best of my knowledge. I understand that if I am found to have provided any false, misleading, or inaccurate information in this registration, or to have failed to provide any requested information, it may be grounds for refusal of the registration.

Signature: _____

Date: _____

VII. Information Release I, _____

___ [Print Name], understand that, in consideration of my registration to be an intermediary with the United States Soccer Federation ("USSF"), the USSF or its hired agent will conduct a check of my background, to include personal data, criminal and civil court indices, personal finances/credit, business status, education, licensure, employment, news indices, professional associations, references, and confirmation of any other information provided in this application. USSF or its agent will report any information which would reflect upon my qualifications for this position. With full knowledge of USSF's intention to investigate and verify the information set forth above, I hereby authorize all individuals, corporations, organizations, institutions, courts, and law enforcement agencies to release to USSF and/or its agent, or their designated representatives, all information that relates to or is requested during USSF's investigation of my qualifications. In addition, I hereby release those individuals, corporations, organizations, institutions, courts, and law enforcement agencies from any and all liability for any claim or damage resulting from the release of information. I also hereby release USSF, as well its officers, directors, agents, representatives, and employees, from any and all liability or claim for damage resulting from the release of the information. In accordance with the Fair Credit Reporting Act and related laws, I understand that I have a right to request in writing a disclosure of the results of the investigation requested, as well as the name and address of the agency who prepared the report.

Signature of applicant: _____

Date: _____

How Does Football Work in the United States and What "Ground" Does a Licensed U.S. Soccer Agent Find?

Once the broker (agent) is registered with the U.S. Soccer, he is formally authorized to act as an agent throughout the United States. Let us now see how the complex endo-federal system of US football is articulated in which the activity of the new intermediary will be carried out.

The sports leagues of the USA are often the best, from a media and financial point of view, just think of the NBA or the NFL with their millionaire businesses and their television contracts around the world, as well as official videogames and a whole series of partnerships from six zeros.

Then why has football been so mistreated in the stars and stripes nation?

The reflection provides us with an interesting starting point for an excursus into the complicated world of North American football, structured in a decidedly different way from that of the old continent and difficult to understand.

First of all: in the United States, there is the presence of multiple leagues, that is, bodies independent of each other, each with its own teams and organization, exactly as happens in almost every other sport played overseas. The UPSL—United Premier Soccer League—in particular is an important league, with a widespread presence in almost all of the United States, but in fact formally considered as an amateur football league and regulated by a body called USADA, which deals with the coordination of leagues' amateur. It is also interesting to note that UPSL is one of the very few American leagues that apply a promotion and relegation mechanism.

The leagues considered as professional, on the other hand, under the aegis of the U.S. Football Federation—the USSF—generally develop their season in *NBA-style* leagues, with a regular season divided into a Conference and a subsequent playoff season. The top two leagues in North America are Major League Soccer (MLS) and United Soccer League (USL). The first in particular is now also known on the European continent given the ever more constant presence of high-sounding names; suffice it to say that only recently have players of the caliber of Pirlo, Lampard, and Kaká closed their career, and names such as David Villa, Alessandro Nesta, and David Beckham have played there.

It is easy to understand that the MLS, despite troubled years and full of changes, is now a reality, and it probably owes it precisely to the combination that is made between football and a typically American sports model, made of sequins, spectacular contours, large facilities, and, precisely, the aforementioned *NBA style* in which it is structured. Not only from the point of view of the division of the season, but also from a purely economic point of view: the clubs are in fact not completely independent but actually belong to the MLS, which controls many aspects from above, including salary caps and costs management. All this in a diametrically opposite way to what happens in UPSL, which sees in all respects a formula more similar to ours, with totally independent teams economically and administratively.

The MLS gave birth to its first season in 1996, exactly 10 years after competitor USL, which itself has still different foundations. In fact, it has several championships under its aegis, all of different technical levels and importance and totally separate from each other, therefore, completely divorced from the logic of promotion and relegation. However, both the teams of the MLS and those of the USL Championship, major league championship, participate in the U.S. Open Cup, the classic national cup also present in European nations. The winner of the latter also participates by right in the CONCACAF Champions League of the Central-North American confederation. The remaining three U.S. teams participating in this event are all from MLS, and are the MLS championship winner, the other finalist and the team that has held the most points in the regular season. While the MLS is not on par with giants like the NBA, NFL, and NHL, it is still considered to be part of the Olympus of the Major Leagues, testifying that it still moves a great deal of money. It is in fact thanks to the MLS that in the United States they have begun to build specific stadiums for football, and the national television coverage with ESPN guarantees great credibility.

In any case, the real flagship of American football is that of women, which has a much higher appeal than Europe and moves unthinkable amounts of money. In fact, the U.S. women's national team can boast four World Cups—out of eight total editions played, including the last in France—as well as four Olympic gold medals. As far as women are concerned, there are two main leagues to battle in the United States: The

National Women Soccer League (NWSL) and the Women Premier Soccer League (WPSL). The NWSL is based on 10 teams, whose winner is determined through play-offs, formed at the beginning of the season with the formation of the rose determined by three factors: a generic draft among all the registered players called *Player Allocation*, a selection method of college football players, very simply called *College Draft* and a traditional system that allows free agency players to be signed. The NWSL has a slightly higher importance than the rival league, which has a different organization: it has first of all a male counterpart, called the National Premier Soccer League (NPSL), and a much higher number of teams, almost seventy, divided into amateur and professional championship. The structure of the championships, in their case, is very similar to that of the NBA, with Conferences divided into divisions formed by a variable number of teams, whose winners compete in the play-offs.

Looking at the vastness of football in the United States, the cliché that sees football as a little-known sport within the continent probably falls away. The path is certainly far from finished but it can be considered well advanced taking into account all the evolutions in the last quarter of a century, including changes in the format and amendments to the regulations, also from. Shoot out to penalties in any tie situation instead of penalties in any tie situation. Although it is not the national sport, in fact, Soccer—as they call it in these parts—has seen an exponential growth in the last 26 years, therefore, from the world championship hosted in 1994, and seems increasingly destined to grow.

The game of football in America is not for everyone.

Soccer, in America, is growing exponentially from an economic point of view.

According to Forbes, 7 percent of Americans cite football as their favorite sport (baseball is at 9%). Since 2012, the MLS has grown 27 percent in interest rate. Founded in 1996, the American topflight has raised the number of its teams to 27—including David Beckham's Miami Football Club International. The American dream, therefore, seems to be fulfilled also in football. What is the cause of this growth?

"I am happy that football in America is growing so fast," said Robert Pires recently.

I think some players like my friend Thierry Henry, Zlatan Ibrahimovic and Wayne Rooney have helped a lot to raise interest in football here. There is a lot of space in America for football. It's not easy to deal with basketball, baseball and American football, but football is for everyone.

Is it really?

Yes, but not in America. It's true: football in America is growing day by day. The women's national team, four times world champion, attracted a large slice of American women's sport. Megan Rapinoe and teammates, however, represent as the inverted mirror of the technical situation of the national team—and of the talent—men.

At the 2019 World Cup in France, the superiority of the stars and stripes women's national team was at times embarrassing.

The United States (the Man's team), whose top players rarely appear in our minds—Dempsey, Donovan, and Howard above all, recently Pulisic and the new Juventus recent signing Mckennie—are struggling so much in the World Cup—on 10 occasions out of 21, the national team has not qualified—as in the CONCAF Gold Cup—where the only accredited competitor is Mexico, the reigning champion.

The Football "Problem" in the USA

The MLS, with its *champions*—all strictly at the end of their career—certainly turned on the spotlight of the show, but did nothing but increase the gap between the stage (the one occupied by the various Pirlo, Ibrahimovic, Villa, Beckham, etc.) and behind the scenes (that of homemade talent).

What are we talking about?

I am talking about Football experienced daily, played in the alleys, that of the streets where the game of ball is prohibited and only finally that of professionalism.

"Here, football is markedly divided into two groups—immigrants and the upper middle class— who interact to a minimum extent. For many of us, including myself, football is [a] relatively new phenomenon. Our parents didn't play. We didn't grow up with the ball and chain."

Says Ryan Huettel[9] who in fact photographs a sharp contrast between two social classes destined more and more not to meet and that historically have not had a culture of playing football as a sport to be practiced in free time. In short, we are talking about a decidedly new phenomenon in the United States. FIFA with U.S. Soccer has tried to stem the phenomenon of dispersion of potential young athletes in other disciplines, with massive investments in the youth sector, in the 0 km growth of new potential talents to be launched in football that matters, but the problem instead of decreasing, it increased.

The more America invests in young people, the fewer young people participate in the game. How is such a paradox possible? Answer: the costs of the academies are too high for the children of immigrants.

With the obvious consequence that at the top of the American pyramid come those with the most money.

Most of the kids who play soccer in America are the children of families that can afford it. The reality is that instead, the United States would be a natural pool of players with enormous potential, such as South Americans or "Latinos" who, however, almost always belong to a low social class, unable to bear the high costs of the Stars and Stripes Academy. Almost all the footballers of the American men's national team come from the richest and most developed areas of the country; to play football, in the United States, you need money. At least in this respect, which is far from irrelevant at a socio-cultural and sporting level, we can say without too many words that soccer, in the United States, is not for everyone.

In a 2015 confession, Jürgen Klinsmann (the then coach of the U.S. men's national team) commented authoritatively on the above problem:

Our national team players have to live and breathe football 24 hours a day. All of this requires a change in mentality and lifestyle. Hearing it from me is funny, but football is self-driven. It is not teachable, unlike other sports.

---

[9] Ryan Heuttel author of "the football times" https://thesefootballtimes.co/author/ryan-huettel/

Self-driven, a word as untranslatable as it is crystalline in its nature: soccer, unlike other sports, is a socio-cultural phenomenon.

Vital elements such as self-play and street football are not part of American society unlike basketball, American football and baseball.

The cultural *lack* of the American sports people in regards to Football, is found from the very first bars, indeed, from the way of defining the sport practiced: soccer; the only nation in the world that felt the need to change its name in order to talk about *football*. An all-American mentality, that of prevaricating and often instituting one's own rules that do not go well with football. Football is and will remain football. Yes, but the USA in Football already has one, and it's not practiced with your feet. A study by Professor Stefan Szymanski (University of Michigan) has shown that the word *soccer* is an English invention. In Great Britain, the use of the term was stopped about 30 years ago. The Americans, with good pragmatism, have kept it to distinguish it from American football. It is a linguistic choice, therefore, a cultural one.

One cannot think of changing a sport born hundreds of years ago. You can't think of making a sport spectacular with pyrotechnic effects, huge advertisements, and bright banners. It would mean violating the very identity of the game of football.

In the last 30 or 40 years, the United States have partially understood this, trying to become homologated to football, like the pure one, born in Europe and played all over the world. The peak of this effort was reached with the organization of the World Cup in 1994, which, however, did not favor the explosion and popular involvement hoped for by FIFA. It must be said that the goal was not to make football the most universally followed and practiced sport (for that purpose, it was enough to expand in Asia and Africa), but perhaps, more prosaically, to find a new economically fertile market in the country. richer, at least in sports terms, on the planet.

Yet men's football is a very popular sport in the United States. As is the women's, however, rich in titles (four times world champion and four times Olympic champion) and which, unlike the men's, in the United States has greater media exposure. It is no coincidence that Alex Morgan got married to Tottenham Woman, also thanks to the delicate situation linked to Covid-19 in the United States.[10]

The very young play football almost everywhere. Kids (and girls) have long known the fun of organizing a game almost everywhere, especially on the grass of the countless parks scattered throughout the United States. Just a ball and a group of friends. A bit like it happened to us when football was mainly played on the street.

Before being a sport, in a large part of the United States, there is therefore the impression that football is still seen as a healthy fun for the very young. Its limit is perhaps just that. The best guys, the athletically stronger ones, do not become footballers. Arriving in adolescence, they end up choosing the most popular sports. Football, basketball, often hockey too, not to mention baseball, invariably engulf the best athletes since high school.

Yet college football is of good quality. For example, in New York, where the author of this text has his American office, there is a famous Academy, which has been part of the Adidas Generation for some years, the Metoval Academy, where the friend and compatriot of the agent author of this text, Giuseppe Rossi, now in the technical staff of Dundalk

---

[10] See https://sport.sky.it/calcio/femminile/2020/09/12/tottenham-alex-morgan-calciomercato-news: "Alex Morgan is a new player for Tottenham Hotspur Women. To communicate it is the same London club through its social channels. The striker born in 1989. Since 2017, she plays with Orlando Pride in the National Women Soccer's League, the top American women's league. Which, however, will only start again in the next spring, which is why the English solution is attracting many players from the States to keep in shape in the meantime. According to reports from the BBC, Morgan would have transferred to the Spurs on loan at least until December. Among the champions of the last World Cup, before her in recent weeks, also Sam Lewis, Rose Lavelle, Tobin Heath, and Christen Press had chosen the Women's Super League. At 31, mother of a girl since last May, Alex Morgan has won everything on and off the pitch. Two World Cups, Olympic gold, the Champions League. With the exceptional score of 107 goals in 169 appearances in the stars and stripes national team. She was the top scorer of France 2019 together with the English White and her teammate Megan Rapinoe, with whom, after the event, she shared intense battle on gender wage equality and women's emancipation in sport. Also taking advantage of a popularity on Instagram of over 9 million followers."

FC (in the groups of the Europa League with Arsenal in the 2019–2020 season, ed.) has brought, together with his colleagues, many U18 boys to local professional football, from NYCFC to the New York Red Bulls. The real problem is that, even if the technical quality present in the U.S. Academy system is all in all good, the players who play it now have an age in which the rest of the world has already exploded at a very high level. The football training system and the school training system in the United States inexorably conflict, leaving the difficult task to the aspiring football player of having to choose between continuing his studies with profit or throwing himself headlong into a system, the football one that in the United States certainly does not give guarantees or appeal like that of other much more famous sports in the stars and stripes nation (basketball, hockey, football). But the audience of players is ethnically very diverse. It is technically valid.

For the public, football remains a marginal sport but with important exceptions that seem increasingly destined to consolidate, which we will discuss shortly.

The reasons for the lack of diffusion of football at the highest level are various, first of all the media presence and pounding of the four sports traditionally most loved by Americans, namely football, baseball, hockey, and basketball, whose calendars are divided equally between the periods of the year in such a way as to always cover the television schedules. The relative less spectacularity due to the acquisitions of rarer athletes than other team sports.

But above all, the scarce inclination to be fans in the sometimes obsessive ways in which we are accustomed in the rest of the world, the true secret of the popular and media diffusion of this sport all over the planet.

The passion does not go beyond the patriotism that they express through healthy cheering for all the national representatives of all sports and in all international events.

The Americans therefore found in the women's national team, beautiful and successful, that identification that is missing in the men's one. Women's football is increasingly becoming a driving force for men's football. Men's football in the United States, which, due to the pool of potential players, organizational skills, and the presence of structures, can certainly produce a national team capable of reaching far more than the quarter-finals won only once in their recent history (Korea-Japan 2002). It must be said that a trend reversal in the last three years from 2017 to 2020 is also and above all revived at the federal level (U.S. Soccer) and in the most representative league such as MLS. In fact, the stars and stripes football has decided to invest heavily in infrastructure. Audi Field, the new home of DC United, was the last to be inaugurated in chronological order. This season, the LAFC's Banc of California has also taken shape and soon Minnesota United will have a new facility ready to use, the splendid Allianz Field. Waiting for Cincinnati, Nashville, and Miami, always waiting for news from New York City and Columbus Crew, here are the Major League Soccer stadiums. We can dream of jewels, from the MB Stadium in Atlanta downwards, in far more noble leagues such as the Italian or French one.

North American football all embraces Ottawa, which becomes the eighth city to enter the Canadian Premier League. The team, which is the league's first historic expansion team, will join as early as 2020 and is owned by Atletico Madrid. The Ottawa team is expected to start playing this April at TD Place and the league has confirmed that the expansion offer has been led by Club Atlético de Madrid, one of the most important brands in the world football market.

"We are thrilled to welcome Ottawa as the eighth team in the Canadian Premier League and Club Atlético de Madrid as the new owners of the Ottawa club," said Commissioner David Clanachan. "We are very excited to launch the club with one of the most iconic and successful football brands in the world and look forward to them taking to the pitch for the 2020 CPL season."

The management of Club Atlético de Madrid spoke through President Enrique Cerezo and CEO Miguel Ángel Gil Marín. "We are delighted to be part of such an exciting project in an extraordinary country," said Marín.

> We would like to bring our experience to a very strong and structured league and we will work with the CPL and the rest of the clubs to contribute to the growth of Canadian football. We want Ottawa football fans to feel proud to belong to the Atlético de Madrid family so that we can start sharing our values with them.

It is clear that football as it is understood in Europe is a phenomenon that in recent years has also been gaining ground in the United States.

A further decisive push for the marketing of brand football in the United States, and its possible equation with European football, where all the top world clubs (and their investors) reside, would be represented by the abolition of a rule, according to the writer, absurd and absolutely unfair, herald of various critical issues in terms of legality with the constitutional dictates of the vast majority of the confederate nations to FIFA, or the peculiar treatment of the non-EU status that all the nations of the UEFA confederation attribute to those players who have not a passport as citizens of one of the 28 member nations of the European Union. Given the limitations on the registration of non-EU citizens, many players from European countries outside the Union, or from outside Europe (such as the United States), often equip themselves with a double passport to have more chances to move from a team outside the EU to a member of UEFA. Each nation of the 28 then adopts its own system of regulation of the aforementioned discipline regarding non-EU citizens, giving rise to a regulatory fragmentation that makes the transfer of a player, for example, of U.S. nationality to Europe, an obstacle race between bureaucratic quibbles, rules to be respected, and effective logistical distances, which certainly make it more difficult for the athlete to be assessed in situ by the scouts and/or technical staff of the European team he intends to purchase, or at least see the player on trial. Here situations such as Pulisic (of Borussia Dortmund) appear more and more like white flies in a context that is strangled from the beginning by an international regulatory system, in the humble opinion of the writer, not in step with an increasingly multicultural and globalized football. Specifically, as regards the Italian Serie A 2019/2020, the regulation, approved by the Lega Calcio on August 5, 2020 regarding the registration of a non-EU football player by an Italian Serie A club is as follows[11]:

- The clubs in possession of the title for participation in the Serie A championship in the 2020/2021 football season,

---

[11] See https://figc.it/media/123378/33-criteri-di-tesseramento-calciatori-extra-comunitari-20202021.pdf

which, as of August 31, 2020, will have more than two professional footballers who are citizens of countries not adhering to the U.E. or to the E.E.E., registered for them definitively, they will be able to register a maximum number of two professional footballers citizens of countries not adhering to the E.E. or to E.E.E., coming from abroad, provided that: 1. one goes to replace their other player from a country not belonging to the E.E. or to E.E.E. that (i) moves abroad, signing a contract with a foreign company, or (ii) whose contract expired on June 30, 2020 or will expire on August 31, 2020, or (iii) who acquires, for whatever reason, the citizenship of EU member country or to E.E.E. or that it has acquired it from January 31, 2020 to the date of publication of this provision; 2. one, without any obligation to replace another player, who at the time of the registration request has been summoned, with inclusion in the match list, for at least two official matches of his national team in the 12 months prior to the date of registration request, or for five official matches of their national team in their career category. The players to be replaced must be expressly indicated by the club concerned and those falling within the cases referred to in points 1 (i) and 1 (ii) will not be able to register for the latter in the same football season. Former Serie A players who have obtained their first professional contract after June 30, 2017 cannot be used for the substitution.

- The clubs in possession of the title for participation in the Serie A championship in the 2020/2021 football season who, as of August 31, 2020, will not have professional footballers who are citizens of countries not adhering to the EU or to the E.E.E., registered for them definitively or will have only one registered definitively, will be able to register, without any obligation to replace another player of theirs, professional footballers from countries not adhering to the E.E. or to E.E.E., coming from abroad, until a maximum number of 3 players from those countries registered for them is reached. The clubs in possession of the title for participation in the

Serie A championship in the 2020/2021 sporting season, which, as of August 31, 2020, will have two professional footballers from countries not adhering to the U.E. or to the EEE, already registered for them definitively, will be able to register, without substitution constraints of another player of theirs pursuant to the preceding paragraph, a professional footballer of those countries coming from abroad, as well as only one other professional footballer from a non-member of the EU or to the E.E.E., on condition that they replace another footballer of theirs from a country not belonging to the U.E. or to E.E.E. that (i) moves abroad, signing a contract with a foreign company, or (ii) whose contract expired on June 30, 2020 or will expire on August 31, 2020, or (iii) who acquires, for whatever reason, the citizenship of EU member country or to E.E.E. or that it has acquired it from January 31, 2020 to the date of publication of this provision. The players to be replaced must be expressly indicated by the club concerned and those falling within the cases referred to in points 1 (i) and 1 (ii) will not be able to register for the latter in the same football season. Former Serie A players who have obtained their first professional contract after June 30, 2017 cannot be used for the substitution.

- The clubs in possession of the title for participation in the Serie B Championship in the 2020/2021 football season will not be able to register professional footballers who are citizens of countries not adhering to the U.E. or to E.E.E. from abroad, nor to register with the status of professional players from those countries already registered in Italy with a status other than that of professional.

- The new members, pursuant to the previous lett. (A) and (B), will only be able to transfer to other clubs in the Serie A championship in the 2020/2021 football season, in the transfer campaign period other than that in which they signed up coming from abroad.

- The clubs that will play the Serie C Championship in the 2020/2021 season will not be able to register professional

footballers who are citizens of countries not adhering to the
U.E. or to E.E.E. from abroad, nor to register with the status
of professional players from these countries already registered
in Italy with a status other than that of professional, except for
the newly promoted clubs in Serie C who will be able to enter
into a professional contract with the amateur footballers of
said countries, already registered for them in the 2019/2020
sports season.

- The numerical limitations on membership for professional
clubs do not concern footballers who are citizens of countries
not adhering to the E.U. or to E.E.E. already registered as
of August 31, 2020 in Italy for professional clubs, without
prejudice to the application of the legislation on visas and
residence permits and what is subsequently provided for
those who intend to assume the status of Junior Series for the
first time.

It is clear that with such stringent regulation, both in number and
in the requirements to be able to register a non-EU player with a club,
every sporting season has very few alternatives. Among other things, this
opportunity is granted exclusively to Serie A clubs, where perhaps the
majority of young American (or more generally non-EU) talents are not
considered ready to play. Allowing an opening to non-EU citizens, at least
for the lower level championships, would certainly allow greater commercial exchange for non-member states of the European Union and a greater
opportunity for young athletes to grow in European contexts with less
media and sports pressure.

Major League Soccer commissioner Don Garber[12] made it clear that
he is certainly full of other ideas and clear objectives: "The league's 25th
season is not an anniversary." Instead, Garber called it a celebration of
all that MLS has accomplished as it moves forward into the next decade.

At a kickoff event for the season Wednesday in New York, Garber
outlined the league's vision for its future, which includes expanding the

---

[12] https://cnbc.com/2020/02/27/major-league-soccer-has-a-25-year-plan-but-
it-needs-to-secure-huge-media-deals-first.html#close

number of teams from last season's 24 to 30 by 2022. Two teams are debuting this season: Inter Miami CF, which is owned by international soccer legend David Beckham, and Nashville Soccer Club.

Garber said the MLS is also preparing for seven new soccer stadiums, better technology infrastructure and continued investment in youth academies in an effort to develop homegrown talent to enhance the quality of play on the field.

The key to making those areas of focus a reality over the next 25 years depends on the money. The plan to increase revenue is simple: Secure multiple and lucrative media deals. The MLS believes the revenue from future rights packages will help sustain its growth as it aims to become a significant player in the U.S. pro sports market.

"The need for revenue will be able to satisfy all the things that all of our critics and all of our supporters want," Garber said. "More investment in players, more investment in infrastructure, more investment in marketing and content, and fan development. The last piece of that for us is media." The current rights package with ESPN and FOX, valued at $600 million for eight years, and Univision, $120 million, generates roughly $90 million per season for the MLS and runs through 2022.

CHAPTER 4

How to Become a Football Agent: Practical Examples

It is not possible, if not from a normative point of view (for which reference is made to the precise reading of the previous Chapter 2), to delimit the boundaries of this profession. In this chapter, however, given his personal professional experience on the subject, the author wants to give a critical and as concrete point of view as possible in the real fulfillment of this activity, trying to answer to the questions which, over the years, have been more frequently placed on him.

The routine of the sports agent is characterized in most of his professional day, by an unspecified series of "contacts" or "connections" with different figures in the world of football: sports directors, technical directors, presidents, commercial area managers and/or club marketing, clients, new, old, and potential. Clients are not only football players, but also coaches and more distantly, entire clubs that directly request the professional services of a specific agent/agency for certain tasks. Moreover, the key role played by the trust component in carrying out this activity is evident, given that the management figures of the clubs who interface with these professionals will then be professionally judged by the management of their home club, based on sporting, promotional and turnover that the *market* meetings with these professionals will have produced.

Trust, it was said then. It is precisely this component that acts as a distinction between a good agent and a mediocre agent. In fact, the companies will be increasingly inclined to reach *Their* agents by telephone, by e-mail, with meetings in person, or through some of their members (coaches *in primis*) rather than using the occasional performances of new agents met perhaps at some meeting organized by third parties.

How to Build Trust: Networking

One of the cinematographic milestones of this activity is a film, now somewhat dated (1992), about the figure of the sports attorney. The title of the movie is Jerry Maguire and a young Tom Cruise, the protagonist, played the role of the young prosecutor.

> *[Jerry Maguire] "I even remembered the words of the greatest sports attorney, my mentor, the great and late Dicky Fox who said:"*
> *[Dicky Fox]: "The secret of this profession is relationships, personal relationships."*

The scenario I'm going to present here is something that really occurred to me with a Serie A club complaining on my mobile phone the impossibility of recruiting an athlete that I had, with my work team, brought from the United States to play in Italy.

> *Giulio, I need you to resolve immediately this thorny situation ... otherwise, you know, the athlete A.M.[1] that you represent ... we must get it started. We cannot keep an athlete who cannot play in the squad!*

The present case concerned the non-granting of the ICT (International Transfer Certificate), which was normally the complete prerogative of the two sports federations of reference within a transfer, which should have had a dialogue with the two clubs (transferor and buyer).

Well, in this and other similar situations, I realized that what is (often) clearly foreseen by the federal and international regulations that I had long studied to obtain the license from FIFA, is often not respected in practice. As in any intellectual profession, however, the unexpected is just around the corner.

With my friend and American partner of Sports Management Worldwide, Dave Knibbs, we had already agreed on everything before. Percentages, commissions, and steps to be followed scrupulously in carrying out the transfer of A.M. were in place; Dave was my only trusted

---

[1] These initials are fictional to preserve the privacy of my client.

contact in the field of women's football in the United States, his agency representing several national footballers, from different nations of the world. The United States, not just any nation for woman football; therefore, the intention to maintain good relations was and must be a priority, especially when it is not me, the football agent, who created a slowdown in the negotiation.

Dave, like all Americans, was not used to this kind of *blame game* made of "It's the club's fault," "No, it's the federation's fault," or "It's the agent's fault." Given the fact that the latter assertion in this case must necessarily be incorrect, given the lack of competence in ICT matters of the agents, the problem was there, and it was real. The English FA, the last federation in which the athlete had played, had not released the ICT and was unable to dialogue, due to "unknown" problems, with the buying club in Serie A.

Let's go back to the quoted request that was addressed to me:

"Either you give us a hand (and you will be the best ... nd), 'or the transfer skips'."

The further problem, if we want, is that the client, whatever role she or he holds, from coach to player, doesn't matter who is to blame. In any case, if the transfer fails, YOU will be the agent not sufficiently capable of making it. So what? Trivially, your client will seek a contractual resolution with you or will wait for the natural expiration of the mandate contract with the agent to go and seek fortune from others.

Of course, painted like this, this profession seems to be really tailored to cynical, unscrupulous people who only look at the best offer. And perhaps in part it is. But this fortunately is only one side of the coin. Completing the anecdote above, it was clear that the outcome of the transfer depended on the concrete opportunity to find some friendly *infiltrator* in the FA, at Wembley, who could help me.

And like the sword of justice, we agents draw our best instrument of attack and defense, which is our cell phone. I quickly scroll through the address book, meanwhile the cellular network did not work much, which in itself is strange in a hyper-technological London where the cell phone often and willingly takes also in the Tube, when I usually go to my office in Covent Garden. With the return of the line, I remembered one of my very first *London friends* whom I met in 2013 on one of my first trips to the UK. He, a man in his 60s, called Ian Anderson, is a (former) football agent, in its original meaning. You must remember that Ian has had to deal with exemplary professionals in his career such as George Weah, Taribo West, and Dusan Tadic, among others. Ian used to go to the training grounds of all the major Premier League and Championship clubs. On the contrary, he told me that it was common practice for the agents to stand in the parking lot at the end of training and try to persuade, a little by acting as a *door to door* salesman, an athlete rather than another to sign with him.

Obviously for me, a child of my time, accustomed to technology, the use of social networking platforms such as LinkedIn and attentive to a scrupulous correspondence via e-mail, his story sounded a bit like a caricature. Or at least certainly not applicable nowadays, where security services, cameras, and clubs are not very willing to receive strangers, make an area like the parking of footballers' cars inaccessible worse than the Cartier vault where part of the English crown jewels are kept.

But Ian (today, I am proud to have him as a partner in my agency, the "Football Factor of Tedeschi & Partners"), with his usual British style, taught me one of the most important lessons in this activity: no telematic contact, however immediate, can ever replace *physical* contact. The meeting in person.

Among other things, when I obtained my FIFA license in October 2013, I was lucky enough to go, through a family friendship, to the office of some sports lawyers, to try to practically learn how to carry out this activity. The CP, FC, and RR lawyers, whom I will always thank, told me about one of their clients, at the time holder of the Italian mayor national team, who had chosen to work with them because one of the lawyers had taken him out to get "croissant and cappuccino, and he had paid for everything!," the player almost marveling at this gesture. Even I, a very young new FIFA agent, I must say, managed to grasp the teaching only in a nuanced way. Precisely because coming from a middle-class family, I received a similar education. When I can, I offer, offering is a nice gesture, a cuteness. Yet, after years I realize how rare it is. It is simply not done in certain cultures.

Returning to Ian, thanks to him, I was able to obtain the coveted ICT in record time, the commission from the athlete and above all a *de facto* certification from the purchasing company, which "if we want, we at the Football Factor of Tedeschi & Partners can reach everywhere." Yes, precisely this healthy presumption of having tentacular ties to be able to contact any club, institution, personality belonging to the football industry was the keystone for this and other negotiations. If you have a low self-esteem or low self-determination, this is certainly not the right profession for you. Still taking up the aforementioned film Jerry Maguire,

"We live in a cynical world, a cynical world.

And we work in an environment of highly competitive people."

So be strongly competitive. But how do you become competitive?

I have created a pyramid of thoughts that have accompanied me and still accompany me in my professional life (and not only). Three corner-stones that guide my daily actions are:

(1) Professional qualification
(2) Diversification and associations
(3) Networking

Professional Qualification

At the beginning of the book, reading the study done by Rossi, Semens, and Brocard, a percentage struck me particularly.

> Overall, 74% of respondents have a university degree. In detail, 41% have a bachelor's degree, another 26% have reached the master's level and 7% have higher qualifications at the doctoral level. The high level of education is combined with a good knowledge of the language. Being key figures in the globalization process of football, agents are required to speak foreign languages to operate in the transnational transfer market.

So almost 75 percent of sports agents have a university degree. Strange if the agent's activity is conceived as that of a practitioner, a person with no particular technical skills, a middleman between clubs and players. It seems obvious that this is not the case. Surely it should be remembered that the peculiar characteristic of the agent's profession presupposes the understanding of a legal language translated into a contract. This fits in well with the (necessary) knowledge of English, in an increasingly globalized market. To date, among us sector professionals, knowing beyond one's mother tongue, English, and another language of your choice, is becoming the obligatory practice.

An example of how football is a multicultural and global phenomenon par excellence, I experienced when a club from the top Chinese division contacted us for one of our assistants, an Argentinian. The meeting, at least the initial one, could only take place electronically, with the unlikely coincidence of times between the EU area where I was operating at that precise moment, Argentina where the player was on vacation with family and China.

To make the negotiation more complex, there was also an evident linguistic barrier that the Chinese world has with Latin or European languages. The result of a Western sovereign ideology, the overwhelming power of the English language and its recognition as a *mother* language in the commercial sphere is something that doesn't sit well for the Chinese. I was informed of this cultural problem, as well as of their particular way of greeting each other, which is always looking toward the future with the expression *"we will hear from you soon,"* by my Chinese collaborator, G. Guochen. In China, he is a *middleman for clubs*. There, as in Qatar or in the United Arab Emirates in general, it is not conceivable at all that an agent who is not presented to the company on duty would propose one or more of his clients.

As in other commercial spheres, in these countries, the way you reach the negotiation is very important. The right presentation of your agency is often essential for the success of the business. Furthermore, South Americans and the Asian world are the polar opposite in the way of understanding football.

In Asia, football is seen in two diametrically opposed variants, without nuances, which never meet: a Chinese club decides to buy a top player (also and above all in terms of merchandising and image) capable of pulling fans to the stadium, otherwise the club decides to focus on the local player (also due to recent government impositions that impose stringent measures on clubs to contain the phenomenon of rampant xenophilia in football, deleterious, according to the Chinese football government, for the entire national football system).

The nuances are typical of us *Westerners*, and I must say, very useful for us agents to try to move the margins of a negotiation on one side or the other. In Asia, the club makes an offer, which, by inquiring about the history of the player and the agency that represents him, it deems appropriate for the athlete. If the offer is refused, or even worse, if the player (or the coach) is hesitant, the negotiation tends to fail. The club immediately turns its attention to something else and, in addition, feels offended for having only wasted time without really having concluded anything. It is clear that in China, football is not a phenomenon that can be compared with that practiced in Europe or, with due differences, in the States.

In the negotiation that I conducted together with my work team, there are all the elements of a complex *school case* when you think that South Americans are usually undecided until the end of the negotiation, they tend to get the best price and have a bond very strong with the family, which makes it difficult for the client in question to decide to move from his homeland. In short: it must be absolutely worth it. There is also a peculiarity in the management of these delicate balances between the parties; the Argentines in particular tend to have large families where all the relatives have a say. Therefore, it often happens that, for an athlete who is already of age, he has to convince his father, mother, brothers or sisters, and even relatives of more distant degrees!

> **Practical tip:** In South America, you need a trustworthy person to rely on in the preliminary negotiation with the athlete's family to prevent any unexpected hitches from proliferating in the middle of a deal conclusion, once the contractual details with the reference club.

As you can see, managing this can be complex. This is why *qualifying* is necessary. Even if the FIFA regulations do not explicitly prescribe the need for a degree, in many internal national regulations (for example, in Italy and France) the individual national sports federations require the possession of a degree in order to exercise, as a precondition for the presentation of the applicant to become football agents.

As well as, even if not formally required, I believe it is highly recommended to have a legal-normative preparation of the relevant sector discipline, both national (where you will want to operate mainly) and international. Not knowing the FIFA, UEFA, CAF, CONCACAF, AFC, CONMENBOL regulations is clearly a big deficit that will not be tolerated by any interlocutor having to do with the agent.

I will go against the trend of what was written by distinguished colleagues who have made the history of this profession by saying this: yes, the degree and any specialized master are fundamental. It is thanks to a specialist master's degree at the Football Business Academy in Geneva (Switzerland) that, in a meeting organized at SoccerEX in Miami (that I attended as a master's candidate) I met my current correspondent from Mexico, Hector Campos, who works in a football territory as complex as fascinating.

Networking alone is not enough. Otherwise I would not have chosen first to follow this path of professionalization. Anyone who wants to sell a product must know about it. And to learn about football, the third sector of the world economy together with entertainment, one cannot have in one's pedigree only having played football for a few years, perhaps in some lower division, thus having *the trained eye* to recognize the new Neymar, Ronaldinho, and Roberto Baggio.

Let's clarify the other concept immediately; to do this job, in 2020, is no longer the agent of footballers but rather *The scout* that identify the talents. Too often, there is a tendency to mistakenly confuse the two figures, disturbing both professional categories. As it is true that the agent, immersed in contracts, phone calls, business trips, sponsorship agreements for athletes or clubs, does not have the material time to be also on the fields and *train* himself to recognize the potential new player to be taken into stable, the opposite is absolutely true; the scout in all likelihood will not know any contractual matters, simply because he is a *field man*, often approached or even paid by football clubs to find new talents.

Studying and working competently is something that pays off. The time of the *factotum* agent is over. Today, most of us agents decide to become corporatized, constituting themselves as legal persons in an agency, where every person included in the company has a specific role.

Diversification and Associations

My second cornerstone originates from this need for specialization and its diversification. Getting your FIFA agent license in 2013 was very similar to becoming a lawyer. You have officially become an agent (or lawyer) yes, but then you have to begin once again. There are no customers, nor are the channels. Network, if you do not have any family history in the world of football, much less. There are basically two ways, and also, these overlap those you have to follow once qualified as a lawyer:

- Look for a *dominus*, an agent already qualified for years who can guide you, or
- Decide to do everything yourself

In whichever of the two paths you find yourself, at the end of the training course, if things have gone well, you will begin to have too many instances to take care of. I said it before and I repeat it, the job of the football agent who lurks in bars or in pizzerias or, as Ian told, in a parking lots, is over. There are now hundreds of tasks to be done every day. Athletes have to be followed in their weekly performances, the agents have to sponsor these performances on social media and put information on websites every week, organize interviews with the media for players or coaches; discuss contract renewals, terminations, and reply to "why the boy plays little? Or, doesn't play at all?"; find sponsors for extra income or simply to make that sporting figure more known in a certain local context. All this, without thinking about the new opportunities to look for with clubs or potential new customers. What about scouting? How can I, as an agent, understand if a client who knocks on my office door is really valid to be represented by my agency? Here then, diversification and associations are fundamental. It is unthinkable to manage all this workload alone. Football is a global phenomenon, and therefore it is very fast. The football industry spins millions of dollars a year, and this obviously attracts the media, always ready to share news first. The advent of social media has also given, if we want, the final acceleration to this profession.

The moment a player manifests his uneasiness through Instagram, Facebook, TikTok, or similar, if you are his agent, you are already late. The company will soon call you, to ask for clarification on *that* post or comment that you didn't even know existed. Associations, I will repeat it to the point of boredom, are necessary. Alone, you don't go far. With this spirit, a series of figures, both professionals and non-professionals, become fundamental pawns in the chessboard of a respectable agency. With these assumptions, I met and subsequently established a relationship of trust with all the members of my team.

I just mention a few:

Claudio Taglialegne (Head of Recruiting per la Football Factor di Tedeschi&Partners)

It was back in 2014 and I was in Lucca, Italy, when I met Claudio Taglialegne, now head of the agency's communication and media area. He immediately struck me for his humanity. At that time, Claudio worked for Lucchese Libertas, a club that played in the then Lega Pro (the third Italian division). I was in town thanks to the honorary president of the club, Giovanni Galli, former historic goalkeeper of the A.C. Milan, above all renowned for being a good person of the Italian football. Between me and Claudio, when we met at the training camp while he was filming the first team during training, a mutual trust was born immediately. Two guys who weren't *sons of someone* but who simply wanted to enter this world.

Needless to say, Giovanni Galli's number ended up in the company's column.

Giuseppe Genovese: (FIFA licensed agent at Football Factor di Tedeschi & Partners)

On September 25, 2013, the day before the FIFA agent exam in Rome set up jointly by FIFA and the FIGC, I found the only friendly face in a sea of sharks. In fact, taking the exam with us, I remember seeing brothers and sons of footballers who played in famous clubs such as AS Roma or AC Milan. Giuseppe, called *Peppe*, is about 15 years older than me, married and with children. A family business to carry on but the dream to turn his passion into reality. Being a football agent. Unlike myself, the time to study the Italian and international sports justice code system was decidedly reduced for him. But studying together day and night, between work and chat together, Peppe managed to pass the exam brilliantly. He is now the person in charge of *recruiting* in our company for all of central and southern Italy thanks to a widespread network of contacts that he has managed to weave over the years by also being a part of the local politics. Further evidence of how the football sector is communicating with other aspects of the Italian and world economy. Our first professional athlete went through Peppe and the player, A.G. who then played in important clubs of Italian football such as Avellino, Sampdoria, and Salernitana.

Daniel Sansone: (Intermediary for the Maltese Football Association e official partner della Football Factor di Tedeschi & Partners)

To give rise to a more international project for my business, a citizen of the tiny Malta island intervened. Just him, married to a South American and therefore very passionate about South American football (from where Malta draws a lot for the purchase of talent not originating from the island) also given the decidedly softer and more permissive federal regulation on immigrants toward them if compared, for example, with the Italian or English one.

Daniel was also looking for new connections through the Internet, to try to get out of an island that does not offer much football opportunities. Currently, however, the most interesting prospect is constituted by a real rising star, Haley Bugeia, a Maltese soccer player managed directly by Sports Pro Management and Consulting, in which Daniel works, and who is a partner of the Football Factor of Tedeschi & Partners. She, just 16 years old, was bought by Sassuolo in women's Serie A, and has already won the award for best player of the month in Serie A in October 2020.

All these examples serve to strongly reaffirm the concept that being agents of footballers is not (anymore) as it was in the past—an activity with an extremely personalistic connotation. If it is done at a high level, the activities in this profession must be scrupulously divided among all the social groups.

Networking

Third and last element that I consider fundamental in carrying out this profession is certainly the Networking activity. This term from the new generation, is actually much more dating back so as to be attributable to the very beginning of the profession of agent. Create your own, recognizable and personal network. A network of trusted contacts is the only way to enter a market sector that is, after all, quite closed, however fast and volatile the nature of every single operation carried out by market operators is. But it is precisely in this *volatility* of the operations that the constant driving force of this activity lies. A continuous turnover of interpreters that guarantees an opening of the market potentially to an infinite number of new players.

The channels to be exploited are infinite; potentially even going to a restaurant to eat a sandwich you can find people interested in interacting with the football apparatus, perhaps by sponsoring small clubs or in more restricted cases, entering the club's social structure. Football is a socio-cultural phenomenon that indissolubly binds all the cultures of the world. Suffice it to say that in the aforementioned United States, the NBA or hockey country par excellence, in New York, precisely on the facade of a huge New York-style brick building, there is a mural of Mohammed Salah, the champion of Liverpool and the Egyptian national team. Or again, that the Brazilian ace Pele has decided to open, also in Times Square, his football store, the "Pele Soccer."

I believe that networking, in turn, can be classified into three different types:

Network through Social Media: In this globalized football, the use of Social Media becomes necessary in the Networking activity. Through LinkedIn, for example, a social network specialized in creating a meeting point between job demand and offer between professionals, I personally had the opportunity to get in touch with professionals of the caliber of world champions Gianluca Zambrotta and Fabio Cannavaro or Bernardo Corradi, former footballer of Lazio and Inter. But the power of social networks, if channeled well, does not end with these high-sounding names. In fact, entire clubs increasingly decide to embrace virtual platforms as a means of meeting new market opportunities, and the reason is soon understood; zero costs in economic terms and very low in terms of time. You only answer who you want, eliminating unnecessary pleasantries. So, for example, with my agency I came in contact with the L.B. member of the technical staff of the Brisbane Roar FC team, a militant club in the Australian top league, where illustrious players such as Robbie Fowler and Alessandro Del Piero have played in various capacities, in a rather recent past. A single large global network that crosses national borders is now possible by endlessly expanding the possibilities of finding new frontiers of entrepreneurial development.

Networking in the old way: surely it is and remains the preferred modality for us agents. Being inserted in certain contexts such as family ones, directly through common friendships, already breaks down the first barrier, that of trust. This is a system that still works a lot in Southern Europe and Latin America. Indeed, we can say that if you are not introduced by the right person, that particular professional sportsman does not get there, or you get there when it is too late. Networking in the old way, however, is affected by the endemic problem of society in which today's football insists; haste. You must always be fast, arriving often before others is essential for the success of a negotiation or simply to establish good relationships before others. Managing different careers going from house to house has become complex.

Networking through official channels: Conventions, gatherings, exclusive meetings are often useful for us agents to get to know the people officially in charge of a task for a specific club. In recent years, the Wycout Forum, a meeting for clubs and agents by now famous all over the world organized worldwide by an Italian company (the brand was recently acquired by Huddle, an American), has been affirming itself, which allows with a sort speed dates to meet more potential clients within two days of work; and SoccerEX, not exclusively reserved for agents, with three editions a year (Europe, USA, Asia) where hundreds of football related companies meet investors and businessmen for possible job opportunities.

How to become a football agent? From this chapter, I believe, we can draw a useful series of ideas, food for thought, and practical cases, which, connected, give rise to two key concepts: networking and professionalization. By themselves, these requirements may not be enough, it always takes a massive dose of luck as in all businesses.

Londoner Richard Brenson, historic founder of the Virgin Group said: "Business requires decision-making cunning and leadership, discipline and capacity for innovation, but also predisposition, irony and, dare I say, luck."

CHAPTER 5

Manage Relationships with the Players' Families, Medias, and Colleagues

Over time, being football agents has increasingly become a job similar to the figure of great managers for important personalities, VIPs, or top politicians, who have an increasingly busy life, sometimes over the top, to allow themselves to manage everything. If we connect the extra football commitments that certain personalities in the world of football have (sponsors, commercials, hosting on TV/radio, etc.), it is clear that the time to take care of other things, weekly trainings and private life excluded, is short.

The Family

Private life, indeed. Too often, the fundamental impact that the family has on the performance of footballers is underestimated. The clubs have understood this very well for 30 years now, providing for hospitalities for newcomers to society. Those just purchased in the last transfer campaign. If there is a term that can be found more frequently in the biographies of footballers when it comes to family, it is *instability*. I too have seen first-hand several times that my clients needed a greater attention to private life when negotiating with a potential buyer club. Trying to understand the complex intra-family dynamics that govern the relationships between footballers, supporters, clubs, and management, we can analyze three concepts:

- **The rebus of the transfer market:** Often, when someone asks me for the first time how the players are doing, my answer is less obvious than expected. "Problems upon problems." And people laugh, incredulous. The reality is easily explained: in major leagues such as the Premier League, La Liga, Serie A or Bundesliga, most players sign contracts for 4 or 5 years. This generates a certain stability within the player's household. Knowing that you can have the same house, the same places to attend, the same club, the same supermarket, see the same people, and so on, gives a certain possibility of planning also to the wives (with any children in tow) to develop an idea of family in that social context. It is clear that children *aggravate the* problem if we want. When footballers with children, come to talk to us at the agency, the first thing they tell us is: "I'm married, I have (for example) two children, if I move, they'll come with me." All this generates, especially at an early age, various problems related to the sudden adaptation of children that must take place in different contexts perhaps in different countries, where different languages are spoken, and at school, the companions you find will never be the ones you left behind. Players and their wives think about this, a lot. And this happens to the lucky ones. The best, the top players so to speak. A decidedly different, more nomadic picture, on the other hand, includes 90 percent of the players who, going to less noble leagues (aka, less rich), manage with us agents, to snatch a contract of 1 or maximum 2 years. And every year, a new cycle opens up. There are, in fact, clubs that are defined by us, market operators, as *selling clubs,* clubs that, according to their philosophy, prefer to take very young boys, unknown to most, and then resell them at exorbitant prices. Two examples above all are Ajax and Atalanta Bergamasca Calcio. A player who passes through one of these clubs, 9 times out of 10 will be sold in a couple of years.

I remember how much uproar the news made in the UK of Manchester United-owned winger Adnan Januzaj who, a few days before being sold to Real Sociedad, had bought a villa in Cheshire for about 3 million pounds. The truth is that the mass media have often ridden the wave of unilateral information, which sees footballers as spoiled rich people, ready only to ask without giving anything in return.

The other side of the coin is that, when a footballer decides (and has the opportunity to do so) to be a professional, he dedicates and therefore somehow grants his life up to 35–38 years to the world of football. Football, understood as an ideological movement, must be good at not spitting out all these players who have failed to become the new Messi and Cristiano Ronaldo, as pawns no longer useful to the system who, in best phase of their life, when other people could have committed to studies or career, decided to run after a ball. Not everyone can make a living from football after hanging up their shoes.

My first client was Samuele Dalla Bona, he played in very important clubs such as Chelsea (with whom he won an FA cup), Milan (of the various Pirlo and Gattuso), and Napoli. Certainly not the last clubs on the market. Well, "Sam," still beloved in London, blues side, one of the most genuine people I have had the opportunity to meet in football, has not yet managed to find his way after having finished his career prematurely due to family problems. Here, the usual family problems.

Let us return to the various Adnan Januzaj cases.

Suddenly your cell phone rings, often on the other side, the sports director of the club where you play tells you: "We have found a club for you, you have to go and do the physical tests by tomorrow." Dozens of calls to the numbers of us prosecutors follow. Personally, I happened to find myself in a situation where a footballer had to come and play in Italy, in Catania precisely, from Finland. Suddenly, the club in Finland decides that they no longer want to give the player the opportunity to move to Catania. I, in Italy, had everything ready, from the welcome at the airport to the car that would take him to the Catania club for the test. From Finland had arrived a more advantageous offer in economic terms for the transferring club, and all the dreams of playing in Italy for this player evaporated in a few minutes of cold international phone calls. Often, we agents and companies, all of us, should remember that the human aspect is never to be overshadowed. We should remember that when we conclude a *transfer,* we are not talking about batches of construction material being transported from one country to another. We are talking of lives, often of very young boys and girls who are changed by mere economic logic. From the perspective of the footballer, most of those who come to professionalism behave as such: exemplary and attentive to economic income. "We have to maximize, Giulio, how many years do I have left to be able to play? What do I do after that? I accept the most economically advantageous offer." The football of 20 years ago, the one made by flags, columns of clubs like Javier Zanetti, Ryan Giggs, Paul Scholes, Paolo Maldini, or Francesco Totti to name the first ones that come to mind, is already a memory. The transfer market is pure business; annual contracts, options for the second year only upon the occurrence of certain stringent conditions, perhaps linked to bonuses, goals, or team placement.

I know players that I have assisted or with whom I have come into contact, who on the last day of the market, for fear of having to change shirts in less than 24 hours, turn off the phone and go into hiding, preferring perhaps to stay six months relegated to tribune so as not to upset suddenly the stability found (for the umpteenth time) of their family. Imagine the state of anxiety with which the players already present in the team, sometimes witness the purchase of their own role of a backup, perhaps praised by the press, or friend of the coach. They know that, from that moment on, everything changes for them, the balance in the team changes.

In the locker rooms, the days of the transfer market, especially in winter, we can see very special things; the tension is evident and sometimes this does not help to manage the already delicate relationships between players, team, coach, and society. In 2019, I had to personally communicate to an athlete who played for Benfica that I assisted, that the club, due to her knee injury, would not renew her contract. That transfer market session was conducted in the spasmodic search for a club for that athlete, because my team and I knew that that contract, that salary, would have been very useful for her economy.

It is in some ways funny when so many football fans from my city, often belonging to organized groups of SSC Napoli supporters, ask me "What does Napoli do? Do they sell Player X? And Y?" When you are inside certain dynamics you know that it is not just a transfer of players. Try to imagine that your father or your mother, year after year, or at most every two years, for about 20 years of your life, are forced to change city and/or country for work. The result is that so many *family* friendships would not exist. Relationships with your relatives, although assisted by the use of social networks, would certainly not be as rooted as those of your classmates, school, university. The players are more and more nomads, and in organized fan groups, almost everywhere, the motto most used is always *only the shirt*. The excessively revolving doors of the transfer market have led most of the top clubs to have a *player welfare* or assistance office to help players and their families find a home, rather than staying in glitzy hotels, but without the heat that a house can offer, with all that this entails. The sooner you put the player in a position to feel comfortable with himself and his family, the sooner he will probably repay you with good performances on the pitch. Happy players generate happy fans, who spend more on matchdays and on merchandise, perhaps buying shirts with their favorite athlete's name printed on them.

The work of us agents is multifaceted. You have to have your hands on everything everywhere; to solve problems of this kind, when they arise, having a widespread network of trusted international real estates can make things easier. Knowing who to contact for apartments, lofts, villas, or houses in the center, can be decisive when determining a negotiation if the club, due to lack of funds or vision, does not have the service for its future new members.

- **Relations with the supporters:** The transfer was successful. We managed to get athlete X to club Y in nation Z. The player makes his team debut. In all likelihood, the good performances help to outline the more or less rapid adaptation of the player within the football reality in which he has fallen by signing his new contract. Leaving aside the sporting aspect, which therefore affects the welcome that the fans at the stadium will reserve for our client, given the visceral nature of the passion for football, especially where it is the most practiced national sport, it is not uncommon to find situations of warm supporters which have a negative impact on whether or not one of our clients stays in that club. Famous is the case of Angel di Maria, when one Sunday evening in 2013, Angel was having dinner with his family at his villa in Cheshire (like Januzaj, Many United footballers are used to buying villas in that area). His dinner was interrupted by particularly troubled fans who tried to access his patio, breaking it, with iron poles for scaffolding. From that moment, Di Maria and his family, frightened by what had happened, decided to go and live in a hotel and after a few months, Di Maria even left Manchester; insiders say the player hasn't felt safe since that event. Sometimes a state of paranoia is generated in the most famous athletes, forced like the VIPs of other sectors, to go around with huge scarves and sunglasses, even in the evening, to avoid being recognized by most. Even in the case of jobs to be done at home, players are not found in their homes very often, delegating these jobs only to people they trust blindly.

  In this context, the agent's activity is very limited indeed. The only thing that can really affect is in recommending the safest area to buy or rent a house, taking information from colleagues who have assisted in the new club of the athlete represented.

- **Health problems:** In this case, we are talking about serious health problems, such as to prevent the continuation of competitive sports. Alas, the Nouri case, a former Ajax jewel, is famous, or, going further back, Stefano Borgonovo suffering from a severe form of ALS. Far more frequent, on the other hand, are cases of serious injuries suffered on the field that negatively alter, and sometimes permanently so, the performance of an athlete. The only attention that we, agents can have in these dramatic cases, is based exclusively on prevention. Try to prepare at least a plan "B" if not also a plan "C," "D," and so on. Anything that is useful to generate new revenue when things go well from a professional sporting point of view is welcome. Many footballers decide at the height of their careers to invest in restaurants, night clubs or discos to be managed obviously by family members or people of trust. In these contexts, the agent can play a fundamental role in connecting his multiple and varied connections, and the footballer who faces the world of non-football business in the spare time from his main activity.

A domestic example is represented by a player with whom I had the pleasure of collaborating from time to time, Sossio Aruta. Sossio was a histrionic footballer, one of almost 400 goals in lower categories, up to the Italian Serie B. Not a trivial matter. He is from Castellammare di Stabia, (Naples), part of all that plethora of players who managed to get to a certain point but not such as to be able to live post career, of what he had earned on the playing field. Perhaps not having the availability to invest in an already consolidated business project, Sossio has chosen the arduous and difficult path of television, successfully participating in several reality TVs such as "Temptation Island" and the "Big Brother," which in Italy have guaranteed him visibility and fame even after his football career was over. Other players, on the other hand, decide, following an injury that seriously affected their career, to pursue other paths but always football related: sports directors, observers, coaches, and even agents. This is the case of an old client of mine, Dapo Kayode, a former Fulham player, who under contract with me moved to Kilmarnock in the Scottish Premier League. Unfortunately, a terrible knee injury has sanctioned his exit from played football prematurely, but Dapo, always characterized by a strong business mentality (he had practically negotiated everything with Kilmarnock, I had the pleasure of going to see his match in the stands that day), decided to take the road to become a football agent and today, he is a friend and a point of reference for several negotiations in local leagues in the UK.

Media World

See Giulio, if you want to work in this sector, the advice we give you is to learn a foreign language and go away, away from Italy. Do you know why? Here are some football dinosaurs who have no intention of giving their seats to rampant youths like you. These dinosaurs are talking to you now.

With these words, the lawyers I worked for immediately empowered me, making me understand that if I stayed in my comfort zone, I would not have a long life. From this awareness, and with the ideological baggage that had accompanied me from the beginning in choosing this activity, in 2015, I opened my first office, paradoxically, not in Italy, from where I started. But in London. Among the streets of the London capital, I used to stop at the stores of the countless clubs in London, each one characterized by its own well-defined soul.

Outside the Chelsea shop, I was able to meet one of the very first people in the world of football that I can now call my friend: Nizaar Kinsella. Nizaar is a Londoner and works for Chelsea TV as well as being a journalist for the famous web magazine *goal.com*. With Nizaar, at the time of the reform of FIFA agents in Intermediaries in 2015, wanted by Blatter and feared by more than half the world of football, we worked together with the president of my Italian association of agents, the IAFA (Italian Association of Football Agent) of which I am a proud founding member, to an article of denunciation against the inaction of the international federations at the time of the transposition of this new, unfair legislation. The article, published on goal.com worldwide, caused a stir and pushed some national football governments to issue an ad hoc regulation that in fact abruptly replaced the FIFA legislation, according to us agents and operators in the sector, seriously penalizing for the proper conduct of our profession. But we have already spoken extensively about this previously. What is important to underline here is how this professional activity is actually very fluid, not easily boxed into unchangeable tracks and therefore lends itself well to being in league with the world of media and information.

Edmund Burke, a deputy, in the House of Commons in a London of 1787 exclaimed a phrase that has become commonplace by now to indicate the real weight and impact that the press at the time had: "You are the fourth power!" Just London today grants, like New York overseas, a series of boundless possibilities of "cross-networking," a networking between different entrepreneurial activities, even for us agents. Thus was born my friendship with the director of London One Radio, BBC supplier, Phil Baglini. Listening to one of his excellent live streams through social media, I was able to appreciate the journalistic slant given by Phil in describing the political scenarios taking place in England at that time, but at the same time I could see the lack, within his radio schedule, of a football program, right in the city of football par excellence! Together we have created a weekly football program of socio-cultural in-depth analysis with themes focused on everything that is football related. From women's football, to social football, from Brexit and how this will affect the status of European footballers in the UK from January 1, 2021, to football as a driving force for other activities. This is an example to demonstrate the infinite potential that social media, media, newspapers, radio, and television can have in being a booster for any kind of activity, even as an agent.

In short, the address book of a sports agent, as well as full of numbers of coaches, sports directors, colleagues and obviously footballers, must also be full of telephone numbers of journalists, it makes no difference between radio, web, and TV. The important thing is that the channels for disseminating news are wide.

From this point of view, social networks help create connections faster; journalists are often the first friends of us agents, because obviously interested in having the news of a transfer of one of our clients first, compared to the competing broadcaster. A journalist market is generated, which it is good not to betray. Once you have chosen your journalist (or your few reference journalists) for that country, it is good to follow them throughout their professional career. A virtuous circle of *do ut des* will be generated centered on loyalty and professional respect. As with Nizaar, so in the United States, my main contact is Roberto Abramowitz, a well-known face in New York and commentator for ESPN and CBS. I met Roberto at SoccerEx in Miami, and he immediately showed his willingness to exchange information between continents.

Colleagues

The figure of the sports agent, as extensively discussed in the previous chapters, is made up of individuals, but increasingly, the high competitiveness of the market and the fast pace of globalized transfer sessions require teamwork. From this point of view, knowing how to manage work relationships between colleagues is crucial. Dealing with local agents, in finalizing an operation, has several advantages from a practical point of view.

First of all, within an international transfer, having ties with a local agent can be of help to know all that series of extra football circumstances that are obscure or unclear to local foreigners. I give an example; political or religious ideologies, customs and gestures to do or not do during the presentation phase with members of the club or the player. In short, it is always useful to have a trusted person who introduces you to the place. The agent's work, however, is characterized by extreme volatility. It is in fact inherent in the nature of this activity, the need for the agent to have to geographically range from one nation to another to find new market opportunities, or perhaps to strengthen old friendships. Among other things, there is an unwritten customary rule of reciprocity according to which "if you help me in your home, I will do the same with you in my home." This solidarity, certainly dictated by the logic of personal interest, however, should not be underestimated in a world as competitive as that of football agents. In fact, associations and corporatism have taken hold at the expense of phenomena of isolationism and protectionism in recent years.

On the contrary, there is an exponential growth of international and national associations that have in fact strengthened the figure of football agents, worldwide.

In Italy:

As a co-founder member, I cannot fail to focus on the aforementioned IAFA (Italian Association of Football Agents) with my friend Christian Bosco as president.

The articles of association read that

> The IAFA (Italian Association of Football Agents) is a non-profit trade association, established on 19 January 2015 and whose essential purpose is to protect the image and rights of football agents as a professional category in relations with the institutions of the state and sports system, as well as the full legal recognition of the relative professional figure, promoting a complete and congenial regulation.

In 2015, in the throes of the chaos dictated by Blatter's deregulation, an innumerable series of e-mails started from the association's institutional mailbox, to try to gather us all under one armed arm, able to face the unjust transience of a qualification legitimately obtained with exam. On April 1 (it really looked like an April Fool), FIFA had eliminated a profession from nothing, replacing it overnight with a new, hybrid figure, that of the intermediary, which had left us market operators in panic. A meager regulation changed the terms in which we had to carry out this activity. We were no longer on the side of the player or the club, one at a time. We should always place ourselves in the middle. With obvious problems related to very clear conflicts of interest. It would have been easy to think that the agent, or rather intermediary, now in the uncomfortable middle position within a negotiation, which could easily dissatisfy one of the two negotiating parties because, if the agent asked for a salary increase for the athlete, the company would be unhappy with his work and, vice versa, the player if his agent had not tried to raise the price. In short, a regulation that did not satisfy anyone.

Following intense battles in the courts of national and international administrative justice, FIFA has retraced its steps, as will be recalled in the already mentioned (see first chapter) future, now imminent, prospects for reform of the profession, a return to the origins essentially. With a lot of qualifying exam and licenses issued by FIFA. In the meantime, however, we agents from various countries have set up our own business, working in concert with local football institutions. In Italy, thanks to the painstaking work of the IAFA, CONI, and the FIGC, we have come to regulate the figure of the sports agent profession, independently, passing to qualify this figure on a state regulatory level, freeing it from the international sports system, too many times influenced by political ideologies that have little to do with this activity.

In England:

The association was created to "promote the collective interests of its member agents and their clients in the world of British and international football."

The AFA was founded by Mel Stein and Jon Smith in 2005 to form a united representative body for football agents in England.

Several important issues at the time, such as tighter regulation of the domestic industry by the FA and growing influence on the game by FIFA, required a "group voice" to promote the interests of sports professionals within the club football. The AFA today represents about 340 professional agents, including myself, having established part of my business in London, I was able to be a member of the prestigious AFA. The other colleagues range from large corporate organizations to small businesses in the transfer market, which is estimated to have a turnover of around £500 million per year. At the heart of AFA's current operations is continuous professional development for its members, ensuring standards are at the highest possible level through training and qualification programs for those new to the industry.

EFAA: European Football Agents Association

Since 2007, EFAA has worked tirelessly to present the point of view of football agents before other football stakeholders: after more than a decade, we show no sign of stopping.

This is the introductory hat that stands on the website of the EFAA well before Blatter's deregulation (the FIFA regulations on working with Intermediaries) with the aim of fortifying the voice of football agents, often unjustly vilified and used as a scapegoat for all the sins of modern football. Attention, with this statement I am not saying that my professional category, myself included, is not faultless. But certainly clubs, federations, and associations were much more represented in the political bodies of the ball. Let's put it this way.

When the FIFA Regulations on working with Intermediaries is enacted in 2015, drastic responses from the EFAA and its members become necessary and no longer avoidable.

The FIFA Regulations have led to the deregulation of the football agent profession, as the previous requirements for passing an exam, signing a code of professional conduct and liability insurance were suddenly eliminated. In the meantime, the application of the so-called minimum standards and its possible implementation only, has been left to the national federations. This led to a chaotic transfer market, as rules and enforcement varied from country to country. The EFAA opposed the deregulation of the sector, leading the organization to act directly on its own. EFAA has since assisted its members in developing accreditation standards for football agents on a country-by-country basis, but with the ability to transfer these qualifications across borders with some sort of reciprocity clause. Each European national sports federation, in fact, had to accept the agents registered in the list of other nations in order to be accepted by its national agents who perhaps had to conclude operations in other countries. This harmonization of standards leads to greater transparency in the transfer market, alleviates bureaucratic difficulties in conducting international transfers and ensures clubs and players the integrity and professionalism of the agent they work with.

The EU sectoral social dialogue for professional football meets and publishes resolutions on intermediaries/agents

In November 2017, the EU Sectoral Social Dialogue Committee for Professional Football, composed of ECA, EPFL (now European Leagues), FIFPro, UEFA, and under the auspices of the European Commission, met to discuss the FIFA Regulation on Working with Intermediaries. This committee noted the apparent defects of the regulations, such as a decrease in the quality of professional services rendered by intermediaries and a fragmented and inconsistent implementation and application of the aforementioned regulation in different countries. Consequently, the committee issued the "Resolution on intermediaries/agents," asking for a *harmonized European approach* in order to "guarantee higher professional and ethical standards." The EFAA supported this conclusion and immediately took action to bring stakeholders together in order to discuss what was needed to bring about positive changes within the brokerage/agent profession, hosting a panel discussion in April 2018 with representatives of leading football bodies, such as the European Commission, ECA, UEFA, KNVB, and Ligue de Football Professional. Likewise, 2018 marked the start of the FIFA Task Force's research on the transfer market, with the intention of reviewing the entire transfer system and current regulatory frameworks (including the FIFA Regulation on Working with Intermediaries). The EFAA has taken an active position in this process, with board members sharing the agent's perspective with FIFA officials in Zurich. While not an official consultation, these meetings represent some of the first real dialogues held between FIFA and football agents regarding the regulation of the profession.

As can be seen, the *good neighborly* relations between the agents of different nations have generated important regulatory changes at all levels. The dialogue and confrontation with the National Federations then led to the discontent of the football system, enriched by unlicensed practitioners within three years of regulatory vacation, up to FIFA, which, taking note of it, decided to reintroduce the figure of the agents of soccer players.

Formal relationships between trade associations and informal relationships made up of commercial exchanges, and reciprocity make personal relationships, once again, the essential element of this profession.

It can be concluded by saying that this activity as a football agent is perhaps one of the most dynamic professions in the world, where human relationships still have a very important specific weight.

Some follow these relationships and those who instead think only of personal gain, an end in itself. Finally, some see that gain as an opportunity to be given to those who, like footballers, pursue a dream, and to give to themselves, to pursue their own, of a dream. As always, clearly, that's a matter of opinion.

About the Author

Gennaro Giulio Tedeschi, born in Naples (Italy), from where some of his ancestors left to seek fortune in New York (United States of America), is a licensed FIFA agent since 2013, now also FA and FIGC Registered Intermediary, specialized in football law, as testified by his law degree thesis entitled: "The football player's agent: legal qualification and discipline of the activity". He is actually working in a sports law firm in Naples, Italy. One of the IAFA (Italian Association of Football Agents) co-founding members since 2015, he is cooperating with various newspapers and radio TV, leading from 2019 to 2021, the program "Football Talks" at the London One Radio, a BBC supplier radio of London. Since 2016, he has been the International lead of the Reality TV Program *Turf Season* helping the new Nigerian football grassroots talents in becoming professionals. CEO and Founder of Football Factor di Tedeschi & Partners SRLS Agency, he is also a member of the AIAS (Associazione Italiana Avvocati dello Sport) that, in July 2016, granted him a certification of specialization in law and economics of sport. One of the attendees of the "Football Business Academy" Master of Geneve (Switzerland), and of the Harvard Business School Negotiation Mastery, Boston (United States). He is directly following the interests of 25 professionals. Currently, he lives in Naples, with operative offices in London and New York.

Index

Agent market and intermediaries
  England, 54
    clearing house system, 39
    English Premier League, 38
    Football Association, 39
    football authorities, 38
    Premier League, 39–40
    UK legislation, 41–42
  France, 51–52
  Germany, 52–54
  Italy
    AGCM report, 45–46
    Beckham Law, 47
    controls, 46
    gallant transfer market match, 44
    Italian Football Federation,
      43–44
    neroazzurro coach statement, 45
    PDP agency, 46
    repatriated workers, 47
    spectacularized market, 44
    transfer market, 43
  Spain
    DSI's investment strategy, 50
    general economic conditions, 50
    Spanish league, 48
    Spanish legislator, 49
Amended regulation, 6–9
American Bar Association's Model
      Rule of Professional
      Conduct, 72
American Civil War, 58–59
Antitrust, 45
Antitrust legislation, 71
Article 81 EC, 5, 6, 8
Articolo 82 CE, 5
Association decision, 6

Bankruptcy law, 50
Beckham Law, 47–49
Blatter reform
  clubs and players, 11

compensation, 12
double representation rule, 10
impeccable reputation, 12
licensed agents, 11
requisites for registration, 12
sports intermediary, 9, 10
Training Compensation, 13
Zurich Federation, 16
Blatter reform of 2015, 35
Bribery Act, 41–42

Canadian Premier League, 96
College Draft, 90
Common law, 42
Competitive imbalance, 72
CONCACAF Champions League, 89
Court of arbitration (CAS), 20

Double representation rule, 10

English Premier League (EPL), 38
European Club Association (ECA), 18
European Economic Area (EEA), 7
European Football Agents Association
      (EFAA), 19, 128–129
European labor law, 26–28

Federation Francaise de Football
      (FFF), 4
Fédération Internationale de Football
      Association (FIFA), 1
  amended regulation, 6–9
  association decision, 6
  Clearing House, 21
  clubs, 13
  deregulation, 16, 24
  Dispute Resolution Chamber
    (CRC), 13
  intermediarie, 43
  licensed footballers, 10–11
  limits, 23
  pay cap, 21

Players Agents Regulations, 31
preparation bonus, 13
public compensation, 21
radical regulatory changes, 9
regulation, 2
Regulations on working with
    Intermediaries 2015, 15
return to the register, 20–21
solidarity fund, 21
solidarity mechanism, 14
Status and Transfers of Players, 13
Statute, 2
transfer compensation, 15
transfer matching system, 19
youth prosecutors, 21
FIFA Regulation on Intermediaries
    2015, 11
Football agent
amended regulation, 6–9
colleagues
    EFAA, 128–129
    England, 129
    EU sectoral social dialogue for
        professional football, 129–130
    Italy, 127–128
    solidarity, 126
consequences, 9
contacts/connections, 103
diversification and associations,
    108–113
European Big Five sisters
    agent licenses, 33–34
    agent market, 35
    bad reputation, 35
    business structure, 34
    Covid-19 pandemic, 35
    English Premier League's
        decision, 36
    Global Transfer Report, 37
    TMS FIFA, 37
    UEFA comparison report, 35
family, 117–122
health problems, 122–124
Historical Excursus
    American Civil War, 58–59
    Calciomercato, 63
    "Cash & Carry" Pyle, 59
    Christy Wals, 59–60

CIES institute, 56
England, 64
entrepreneurial category, 55
football observer, 60
France, 61–62
German federation, 61
Gigi Peronace, 63
intermediaries, 57–58
UEFA match agent, 63
UEFA system, 64–65
UNFP, 64
International Federation, 3
legal evolution, 3
media world, 124–126
Multiplayers International
    Denmark, 5
networking, 114–116
original regulation, 3–6
Piau's complaint, 4
professional qualification, 107–108
recognition, 2–9
regulation, stepping stone, 1
supporters, 122
trust building, 104–107
Football Association (FA), 39
Footballer's Status Commission, 4, 7
Football Stakeholders Committee,
    17–18, 29, 30
Football training system, 95
France Football Federation (FFF), 18
Free all policy, 16
Future Reform Prospectuses
    Clearing House, 20
    European Football Agents
        Association (EFAA), 19
    FIFA TMS, 19
    Football Stakeholders Committee,
        17–18
    France Football Federation, 18
    Italian national football system, 22
    mandatory liability insurance, 19
    new Agents Regulation, 19
    relations, 24–26
    Sports Order, 22
    temporary football agents, 26–28

Gallant transfer market match, 44
GEA World Agency, 45

Globe Soccer meeting, 19

Hamburger Sport-Verein, 53
Harmonized European approach, 130
Health problems, 122–124

Impeccable reputation, 6, 12
Insolvency law, 50
Instituto Superior de Derecho y
    Economía (ISDE), 32
Intermediary concept, 31
International Center for Sports
    Studies, 56
Italian Association of Football Agents
    (IAFA), 127–128
Italian Football Federation, 43–44
Italian national football system, 22

Licensed agents, 11

Major League Soccer (MLS), 89
Media world, 124–126
Minimum Standards, 16, 69
Minimum standards, 69
Model Rules of Professional Conduct,
    71
Multiplayers International Denmark,
    5

National Collegiate Athletic
    Association (NCAA), 68
National Conference of
    Commissioners on Uniform
    State Laws (NCCUSL), 68
National Premier Soccer League
    (NPSL), 90
National Sports Federation, 10, 13
National Union of Professional
    Footballers (UNFP), 52
National Women Soccer League
    (NWSL), 90
Networking, 114–116

Player Allocation, 90
Players and clubs, 4
Player welfare, 121
Premier League, 39–40
Professional liability insurance, 7

Professional qualification, 107–108

Regulations on the Status and Transfer
    of Players (RSTP), 40

School training system, 95
Social dumping, 27
Solidarity contribution mechanism,
    14
Solidarity fund, 21
Spanish tax reform, 48
Spectacularized market, 44
Sports Agent Responsibility and Trust
    Act (SPARTA), 70
Sports intermediary, 9
Sports Justice, 22
Summary model, 25

Temporary football agents, 26–28
Third-party ownership (TPO)
    agreement, 39
Transfer matching system, 19, 37
Trattato di Roma, 5
Treaty of Rome, 5

UEFA European Clubs Forum, 18
UEFA system, 64–65
UK legislation, 41–42
Uniform Athlete Agents Act (UAAA),
    68, 69
Union of Professional Football Clubs
    (UCPF), 52
United Premier Soccer League
    (UPSL), 88
United Soccer League (USL), 89
United States Soccer Federation
    (USSF), 75
United States Sports Agent
    antitrust legislation, 71
    competitive imbalance, 72
    figure, 67
    football "problem"
        Alex Morgan, 93–94
        all-American mentality, 93
        brand football marketing, 97
        football training system, 95
        Italian Serie A 2019/2020,
            97–100

Klinsmann's comment, 92
Ottawa team, 96
school training system, 95
self-play and street football, 93
Intermediary Declaration, 75–76
   legal persons, 82–84
   memorandum, 77–78
   natural persons first name, 79–81
   requirements for, 76
licensed soccer agent, 88–91
minimum standards, 69
model, 69
NCCUSL, 68
North American perspective, 71
SPARTA, 70, 72

state-based regulation, 74
UEFA confederation, 73
Uniform Athlete Agents Act, 68, 70
U.S. Soccer Federation
   Intermediary Registration
   Form, 85–87
U.S. Football Federation (USSF), 88
U.S. Soccer Federation Intermediary
   Registration Form, 85–87

Women Premier Soccer League
   (WPSL), 90
World Football Federation, 9

Youth prosecutors, 21

OTHER TITLES IN THE SPORTS AND ENTERTAINMENT MANAGEMENT COLLECTION

Lynn Kahle, University of Oregon, Editor

- *Inside the World of a Football Agent* by Gennaro Giulio Tedeschi
- *The Business of Music Management* by Tom Stein
- *The Olympic Sports Economy* by Max Donner
- *Great Coaching and Your Bottom Line* by Marijan Hizak
- *Artist Development Essentials* by Hristo Penchev

Concise and Applied Business Books

The Collection listed above is one of 30 business subject collections that Business Expert Press has grown to make BEP a premiere publisher of print and digital books. Our concise and applied books are for…

- Professionals and Practitioners
- Faculty who adopt our books for courses
- Librarians who know that BEP's Digital Libraries are a unique way to offer students ebooks to download, not restricted with any digital rights management
- Executive Training Course Leaders
- Business Seminar Organizers

Business Expert Press books are for anyone who needs to dig deeper on business ideas, goals, and solutions to everyday problems. Whether one print book, one ebook, or buying a digital library of 110 ebooks, we remain the affordable and smart way to be business smart. For more information, please visit www.businessexpertpress.com, or contact sales@businessexpertpress.com.

www.ingramcontent.com/pod-product-compliance
Lightning Source LLC
Chambersburg PA
CBHW061325220326
41599CB00026B/5037